Florida's Museums
and
Cultural Attractions

Second Edition

Murray Laurie and Doris Bardon

Pineapple Press, Inc.
Sarasota, Florida

Inquiries should be addressed to:

Pineapple Press, Inc.
P.O. Box 3889
Sarasota, Florida 34230

www.pineapplepress.com

Library of Congress Cataloging-in-Publication Data

Laurie, Murray D., 1934-
  Florida's museums and cultural attractions / Murray Laurie and Doris Bardon.
-- 2nd ed.
      p. cm.
   Includes index.
   ISBN 978-1-56164-408-7 (pbk. : alk. paper)
   1. Florida--Guidebooks. 2. Museums--Florida--Guidebooks. 3. Historic sites-
-Florida--Guidebooks. 4. Gardens--Florida--Guidebooks. I. Bardon, Doris,
1919- II. Bardon, Doris, 1919- Florida's museums and cultural attractions. III.
Title.
   F309.3.B365 2008
   917.5904'64--dc22
                                             2008008786

First Edition
10 9 8 7 6 5 4 3 2 1

Design by Shé Heaton
Printed in the United States of America

Contents

Introduction

Welcome to Florida and to the abundance of unique cultural treasures that awaits you. Whether you are a newcomer, a tourist, or a longtime resident, you will find museums and cultural centers to enchant, educate, and amaze you and make your visit memorable.

To help you find your way, we have included a few maps and for each listing you will find the address, phone number, and such basic information as hours of operation, admission fee, special features, and parking, as well as a brief description. The attractions are arranged geographically, but there is a complete alphabetical index to help you locate specific museums, historic sites, theaters, and performing arts centers as well as special types of museums and attractions. In general, we have listed only attractions that are open to the public on a regular basis as of 2008, with schedules of exhibitions and performances.

Be prepared for surprises. There is more to Florida than beaches, theme parks, and shopping malls. Leave the major highways and discover roads canopied with giant oak trees, cattle and horse ranches, citrus groves and botanical gardens, romantic ruins and rustic villages. Treat yourself to an outdoor concert under the stars, a folk festival, a crafts fair, a historical re-enactment, or an ethnic gathering at some of the cultural attractions we describe. We found the Florida Association of Museums, Inc., website (www.flamuseums.org) particularly helpful because it is arranged geographically, as this book is, and can alert you to exciting things going on in museums around the state.

Since the last edition of our Florida museums guide, published in 1998, new museums and cultural attractions have opened and many have expanded. The increasing public interest in nature and ecology has prompted us to include sites that feature the outstanding natural wonders of this state. We invite you to use this guide to find attractions that the average tourist on a whirlwind theme-park itinerary misses entirely.

As we traveled the state visiting and revisiting all of the sites we write about, one of our most rewarding experiences was meeting and talking with museum directors, guides, and volunteers. They are eager to share their enthusiasm and knowledge with you as well.

We were frequently reminded that the history of Florida predates the landing of the *Mayflower* in

New England. Throughout the state, archaeological studies are under way, revealing Florida's history in ever greater depth. To travel through Florida's historic and cultural sites is to set sail on a voyage through time. A visit to a restored village of the late 1800s evokes nostalgia for the way things were. But when you visit a contemporary science museum, you come face to face with modern reality.

Although we do not critique or rank the attractions, we do try to give you our impressions and pass on information about the special features each has to offer. Many of the attractions will induce you to linger, so allow yourself plenty of time to absorb their full flavor. The guide is designed to make it easier for you to plan an afternoon excursion, to see several attractions that might be within walking or close driving distance, or to stay over several days to take full advantage.

We were delighted to find that many of the attractions we visited now print their brochures in several languages, reflecting an increase in tourism to Florida from abroad; some have also provided multilingual signage for exhibits and displays. If you are planning a visit with a group of international visitors, inquire about having a guide in your group's language of choice.

Some of us like to strike out for adventure on the spur of the moment. Keeping a copy of this guidebook in your car will help you find delightful diversions as you journey through Florida.

Others prefer to plan ahead, mapping out excursions with precision and gathering plenty of information beforehand. This guidebook can lead you to out-of-the-way surprises as well as to blockbuster museums, alert you to special features, let you know if you need to pack a lunch or if there is a café on site, tell you whether you can stock up on gifts and souvenirs, and help you avoid the disappointment of arriving on the one day of the week when the museum is closed.

Most Florida counties support visitors' and convention bureaus or offices that can supply colorful brochures and other materials for general or specific interests. Such local resources are especially helpful if you are planning a trip for a group.

We have provided a list of contacts for your convenience. And for those addicted to finding the latest nuggets on the Internet, there is museum-related material on-line. Following the list of contacts, we have included a few websites we have found to be helpful for up-to-date news of exhibits, programs, and special events. Increasingly, you will find websites for specific interests that will alert you to new offerings.

It is not surprising that museum-goers also enjoy festivals. In Florida there is a festival for almost every weekend of the year, often centered on local culture and heritage. In the fall and spring the festival calendar explodes. We celebrate art, rattlesnakes, seafood,

pioneers, bluegrass music, ethnic
cultures, peanuts, kites, wine,
jazz, manatees, and on and on.
Keeping up with Florida festivals is
a challenge to the most dedicated
gadabout. Weekend entertainment
supplements published by most
Florida newspapers do an
admirable job of providing details
about local cultural attractions
and events.

Florida Historical Highlights

The ebb and flow of history has deposited a jumble of fascinating artifacts on Florida's shores and in its inland fields, forests, and waterways. We discovered many of these from the panhandle to the Keys. Some were as massive and well known as the Castillo de San Marcos in St. Augustine. Others were as subtle and evocative as a collection of turpentining tools, a moonshine still, and turn-of-the-century kitchenware in a small county historical museum in Live Oak.

The tide is rising again, awash with the sediment of towering glass-walled condos, exotic theme parks, and overburdened landfills—the middens of our modern culture.

As a kindness to those new to Florida, or to those who believe that nothing much happened here between the founding of St. Augustine and the construction of Walt Disney World, we offer a key to historical sites and museums presented in this book—the material culture that is the true heritage of the state.

Life was good for the peoples who lived in Florida before Spanish adventurers discovered it. Resourceful native Floridians built massive mounds of shells and sand to elevate their temples, lived in large settlements or hunting camps as the circumstances required, and created elegant and serviceable pottery and tools perfectly adapted to their aesthetic and practical needs. Look for evidence of their lifestyles at the Crystal River Archaeological Site, the Lake Jackson Indian Mounds near Tallahassee, and displays in museums all across the state.

Splashing ashore with their horses and dogs at such a likely spot as the DeSoto National Monument west of Bradenton, the men of Spain entered a world as alien to their own as astronauts found on the moon. These early encounters were disastrous for the natives of Florida, signaling the end of their way of life. The armor-clad invaders were only the first wave of the future: soldiers, administrators, missionaries, artisans, you, me.

Florida derives its name from Pascua Florida, the Spanish "Feast of Flowers" at Easter. In his quest for gold and the legendary "fountain of youth," Juan Ponce de León sighted the coast of Florida in 1513, close to the day on which Easter was celebrated. Although he never found gold treasure or the famed fountain, he had discovered a new land and given it a name.

In 1565, the Spanish established St. Augustine, the first permanent settlement in what would come to be called the United States of America. Their next settlements included Pensacola and mission outposts in the northern interior. Search them out in living history programs in the Spanish Quarter in St. Augustine, at Fort Barrancas in Pensacola, and at the Mission of San Luis de Apalachee site in Tallahassee. France had a toehold at Fort Caroline near Jacksonville, but the Spanish saw no reason for diplomacy and slew the French there and at bloody Matanzas Pass, site of the little coquina blockhouse built to guard the Spanish colony's southern flank near present-day St. Augustine.

The tournament of imperial rivalry in Europe pitched Florida to England near the end of the eighteenth century, opening up new opportunities for British colonists. British artifacts mingled with and sometimes submerged Spanish material culture in St. Augustine, but the layers are revealed at such sites as the Oldest House in St. Augustine and the Kingsley Plantation on Fort George Island, north of Jacksonville.

Northern Florida became a safety valve and an escape route for Native American tribes pushed out of Georgia and Alabama and for slaves fleeing harsh plantation life, and a haven for pirates and traders. The confusing overlap of these interests is admirably interpreted at the San Marcos de Apalache State Historic Site in St. Marks, south of Tallahassee.

Florida became Spanish again between 1784 and 1821, but then Andrew Jackson marched into Pensacola, ending Florida's role as a territorial beanbag tossed between bargaining nations. It was acquired by the United States in 1821, with Tallahassee chosen as the capital—halfway between St. Augustine and Pensacola, the capitals of east and west Florida. The frontier village evolved into a well-appointed seat of political power, as can be discovered in the Old Capitol building in Tallahassee.

Meanwhile in the Keys, wreckers were making their fortunes salvaging the spoils of ships dashed on treacherous reefs and shoals. Key West was for a time the richest city in Florida, as you will discover in the museums, brick warehouses, and elegant homes—the latter exemplified by the Oldest House in South Florida, and the red brick Customs House, still beautifully preserved today.

Sugar planters moved into the fertile lands along the Gulf Coast and the Atlantic rim south of St. Augustine early in the nineteenth century. The Gamble Plantation near Bradenton evokes this period, as do the ruins of sugar mills at Bulow Plantation Ruins Historic State Park, all but destroyed in the Wars of Indian Removal in the 1830s and 1840s. The Dade Battlefield commemorates an event in 1835 that sparked the Second Seminole War, a woeful series of skirmishes, broken promises, and tragic events. The war spread southward, and in 1840 Seminoles wiped out Jacob Housman's town on Indian Key, now a state historic site.

Although thousands of Seminoles were sent to Oklahoma, several hundred others faded into the impenetrable Everglades, thus preserving their culture and way of life. Visit Ah-Tha-Thi-Ki Museum near Clewiston to meet the Seminoles on their own grounds.

In 1838 and 1839, Floridians seeking statehood met in Port St. Joe in the Florida panhandle, where the Constitution Convention State Museum is now located, but statehood was not granted until 1845. Plans were soon under way to develop roads and a railroad system. One of the most ambitious was the Florida Railroad, linking Fernandina and Cedar Key, which was completed in 1861. Museums in each of these cities will fill you in on the role of David Levy Yulee, the state's first railroad baron.

The federal government began to take an interest in coastal defense, building a series of lighthouses and improving harbors around Florida's perimeter. Lighthouses erected during this time can still be seen in St. Augustine, Jupiter, Key West, St. Marks, and other prominent sites, and museums devoted to lighthouses can be seen in St. Augustine, Ponce Inlet, and Key West. Forts were also constructed: Fort Zachary Taylor was built in Key West to guard the busy port; Fort Pickens protected Pensacola's harbor; and Fort Clinch was begun in Fernandina. During this period, Dr. John Gorrie made a most important contribution by

inventing an early version of the air conditioner to cool his fever patients: a model can be seen in the John Gorrie Museum in Apalachicola.

All of this progressive activity ended abruptly when Florida joined the Confederacy in 1861. Although port cities from Pensacola to Fernandina were in Union hands, the interior belonged to the Confederate cause. The major battle to protect that cause was fought in 1864 at Olustee, preserved at the Olustee Battlefield Historic Site east of Lake City, where the battle is faithfully reenacted each February.

After the Civil War ended in 1865, railroad tycoons began laying a web of steel tracks all over the landscape. Henry Flagler built grand hotels such as the Ponce de León (now Flagler College) in St. Augustine, and Henry Plant challenged him with the even more exotic Tampa Bay Hotel. Flagler set the style for the Gold Coast with Whitehall, his mansion in Palm Beach, and Plant's taste for European and Oriental decor can be appreciated in the Henry B. Plant Museum in Tampa. The railroad era left us with another bonus. Many of the charming, centrally located depots and stations have been recycled into local museums.

Millionaires found Florida a compatible place to spend the winter and indulge their tastes for extravagant homes in the early twentieth century. In Sarasota, circus mogul John Ringling built the Venetian-style Cà'd'Zan

("House of John"), his personal residence, along with a separate Renaissance palace to house his art treasures. James Deering transported trappings of sixteenth-century Europe to embellish the elaborate gardens and buildings of Vizcaya, his estate overlooking Biscayne Bay in Miami. Much simpler but just as fascinating are the winter homes of Thomas Edison and Henry Ford in Fort Myers.

In the meantime, life went on for Florida's simple working folk: the farmers and fishermen, cow hunters and ranchers, turpentiners and phosphate miners, cigar makers and shopkeepers, spongers and orange pickers. Their stories are told in the Museum of Florida History in Tallahassee, the Forest Capital Museum in Perry, the Ybor City Museum, the Museum of Industry in Pensacola, and all the county and regional museums that preserve and interpret Florida's local heritage.

Buildings tell a story of the past, too. Pleasing assemblages of historical structures can be visited at Heritage Park in Largo, the Pioneer Florida Museum in Dade City, the Tallahassee Museum, Manatee Village Historical Park near Bradenton, and the Pioneer Settlement in Barberville. These time capsules gently take you back to the past as soon as you step over the threshold of a Cracker cabin, a country church, or a one-room schoolhouse.

We invite you to explore on your own, picking and choosing your route along the time line of Florida history, discovering new ways to see and understand the rich and diverse heritage of our state.

Pathfinders of Florida

On our quest to discover a variety of museums and historic sites in Florida, we followed the tracks of some visionaries who guided us to new insights about our remarkable state. They left their impressions in their eloquent words and in their art, giving us a deeper appreciation and understanding of Florida: its past, present, and future.

The Florida of the Inca is a classic sixteenth-century narrative of the expedition of Hernando de Soto, written in a direct, you-are-there style. It was compiled by Incan writer Garcilaso de la Vega from first-hand accounts of the survivors of de Soto's ill-fated trek through Florida in 1539.

The gentle Quaker botanist William Bartram left vibrant descriptions of the world he observed along the St. Johns River and across the broad savannas of middle Florida in 1784. Luckily, we can still see some of these same views spread before us, as on Paynes Prairie near the former town of Cuscawilla (now Micanopy), where Bartram was the guest of Chief Cowcatcher. He recorded this encounter in *The Travels of William Bartram*.

John James Audubon's monumental *Birds of America* made him famous, justifying his arduous travels and the painstaking artistry

of his drawings. He visited Florida in the 1830s, sketching such birds as the pink flamingo and the great white heron, never seen before by most of the world.

Writer/naturalist John Muir was on a thousand-mile hike when he reached Florida in the late 1860s. He struggled through swamps and forests and was laid up with malaria for a time in Cedar Key. He later wrote of his trek, carefully describing the flora and fauna he saw and the people he met.

Southern poet and writer Sidney Lanier visited Florida in 1876 and described the countryside, social life, and hospitality he enjoyed. He published his enthusiastic impressions in one of the state's earliest tourist guides, *Florida: Its Scenery, Climate, and History.*

Serene and expansive views of life on the upper St. Johns River in the late 1880s were captured by amateur photographer Leonard Dakin. He recorded the era of Florida's first orange boom from his family's grove at Racimo, south of Palatka. Picnics, passing steamboats, boating parties, and Victorian gentlefolk in semitropical surroundings are favorite themes of his pictures.

Artist Martin Johnson Heade, renowned for his exquisite paintings of birds and orchids, settled in St.

Augustine in the 1880s with Henry Flagler as his patron. He painted our native trees and plants and a number of splendid atmospheric scenes of Florida sunsets and swamps.

The magazine *Harper's Weekly* sent Frederic Remington to Florida in 1895 to write and illustrate a story on the Cracker cowboy. His honest sketches of Florida cowmen at work revealed the hardships of the Southern frontier rather than the glamour of the American West.

Winslow Homer came to Florida in the 1890s to paint and to fish. His quick, fresh sketches and watercolors show an angler on the Homosassa River, a long white boat on the St. Johns River, and the fishermen of Key West— Florida as seen through the eyes of a sophisticated sportsman.

Luminous landscapes of turn-of-the-century Florida by visiting German artist Herman Herzog perfectly capture the elusive atmospheric enchantment of our coastal beaches, inland rivers, and secluded hammocks. Some of his finest works are in the collection of the Harn Museum in Gainesville.

James Weldon Johnson has been called one of Florida's Renaissance men. The gifted African-American poet, novelist, songwriter, and newspaperman composed "Lift Every Voice and Sing," the Negro anthem, in the early 1900s.

After World War I, Addison Mizner introduced the Mediterranean-revival style to Palm Beach, epitomized by his design for the Everglades Club with stucco walls, red tile roof,

and wrought iron grillwork. Wealthy patrons commissioned him to create palatial oceanfront estates with courtyards and towers, pools and fountains, galleries and arcades, and other Spanish elements that defined Florida architecture for decades to come.

Zora Neale Hurston was an anthropologist, folklorist, novelist, and playwright. Her tales of growing up as a young African-American child in Eatonville, near Orlando, are full of the humor, warmth, and pain of a kindred human spirit, as are her stories set in juke joints, cane fields, and turpentine and migrant labor camps.

In the 1920s, editor, author, and philanthropist Edward W. Bok created a sanctuary for wildlife in Lake Wales, a garden filled with beautiful trees, flowers, and a magnificent singing tower as a gift to the American people. The talented Dutch immigrant had prospered in his new homeland, and he left this as his lasting legacy.

During the Great Depression, artists were commissioned to paint murals in federal post offices all over the nation. Those in Florida reflect community life and work such as cotton harvesting in Madison and cypress logging in Milton, or they depict panoramic historical scenes as in the Tallahassee and Miami Beach post offices.

Thousands of photographs of Florida people, landscapes, and news events were recorded by the Burgert Brothers, commercial photographers in Tampa between 1918 and 1963. Skillfully composed and carefully documented, these images, now in the collection of the Tampa Public Library, illuminate life in Florida during the first half of the twentieth century.

Marjorie Kinnan Rawlings wrote with great candor and affection about her neighbors in Cross Creek and of folks in the Big Scrub wilderness near Ocala. Her rich images of Florida Cracker life can be found in *The Yearling, Cross Creek,* and her other books, some of which have been made into successful films.

Marjory Stoneman Douglas revealed the mysteries of the Everglades in *The Everglades: River of Grass.* She wrote with the keenly observant eye of the newspaper reporter she was, and she became a passionate defender of this fragile and threatened wilderness.

He loved fishing, cockfights, swapping stories at the local bar, and the free and easy life in Key West. Ernest Hemingway did some of his best writing when he lived on the island in the 1930s and 1940s, stamping his indelible imprint on Florida's southernmost city.

Everyone's still looking for that cheeseburger in paradise and that lost shaker of salt in Margaritaville, thanks to singer/songwriter Jimmy Buffet. With music and lyrics he evokes the magical, kaleidoscopic, sunstruck vision of tropical Florida that we all hope to find someday.

1.

Northwest Florida

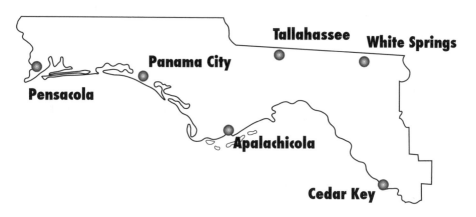

Pensacola

A colorful, richly textured historical fabric overlays this port city at the western end of Florida's Panhandle, and new discoveries continue to illuminate the bold, multidimensional pattern. The discovery and investigation of Don Tristan de Luna's Spanish ship that sank in the harbor during a hurricane in 1559 adds another dimension to the story of colonial Pensacola. A series of forts defines the importance of the military presence—from the French and Spanish garrisons, to Civil War engagements, to the modern U.S. Navy. Archaeological sites, houses, commercial buildings, and civic structures reveal the lives and times of the resident community from prehistoric times to the present. Pensacola claims settlement earlier than St. Augustine and has recreated its historic past in a casual, friendly,

accessible fashion. One could easily spend several days taking in the museums and restored buildings at Florida's western gateway.

Historic Pensacola Village

Address: 205 East Zaragoza Street
Pensacola, FL 32501 (Tivoli
House)
Features: Museum shop, guided
tours
Hours: Monday-Saturday 10-4
Admission: Tours and admission to
all village sites, adults $6, stu-

dents and seniors $5, children aged 4–16 $2.50 (tickets are available at the Tivoli House or at the Wentworth Museum on Jefferson Street)

Parking: Free village parking at Zaragoza and Tarragona Streets

Phone: 850-595-5985

Website: www.historicpensacola. org

E-mail: info@historicpensacola.org

This living history museum complex, located in the Seville Historic District, brings the rich heritage of the Gulf coast of Florida to life with its diverse mix of historic buildings. Stroll down narrow brick sidewalks past restored frame cottages, some now used as shops and restaurants. Examples of authentic Gulf coast architecture, influenced by Caribbean, French, and Spanish building styles, span two hundred years. Follow the Colonial Archaeological Trail signs throughout the village for a broader vision of human impact on this area. The all-inclusive admission fee invites leisurely exploration of the village.

The Tivoli High House
205 East Zaragoza Street

The public guided tours begin at this reconstructed structure. The two-story galleried building built by French carpenters in 1805 symbolizes the diversity of Pensacola's history. It served as a gambling house and dance hall during the Spanish period, which offended the staid Americans who

followed, and then was turned into a hotel for Union soldiers during the Civil War, only to be demolished in the 1930s. It was rebuilt as an exact copy on its original site as a Bicentennial project in the 1970s.

Manuel Barrios Cottage
209 Zaragoza Street

This small frame cottage contains two room vignettes and a central exhibit area devoted to life in west Florida in the 1920s.

Museum of Commerce
Corner of Zaragoza and Tarragona Streets

Glimpse turn-of-the-nineteenth-century downtown Pensacola in this reconstructed streetscape depicting actual businesses such as the newspaper and print shop, a hardware store, and a music store. Visitors can window-shop along the avenue and climb aboard the trolley to savor the diversity of the port city's commercial district.

Museum of Industry
200 East Zaragoza Street

Fishing, lumbering, brick-making, and railroading brought riches from the sea and the forests as Pensacola grew. This museum depicts the stories of the snapper-fishing fleet, the lumber boom, and the growth of the port and railroad with exhibits, models, and authentic equipment.

Julee Cottage
210 East Zaragoza Street

One of the oldest houses in Pensacola, this simple but elegant cottage built before 1805 was owned by a free woman of color, Julee Panton. Exhibits inside focus on the role of African Americans in the history of West Florida from 1527 to the early twentieth century.

Lavalle House
205 East Church Street

This typical French Creole house is furnished with authentic eighteenth- and nineteenth-century antiques, which help to bring alive frontier life in the early 1800s. The focus of the Village's living history program is located here, with demonstrations of colonial life and crafts.

Quina House
204 South Alcaniz Street

This early nineteenth-century, French-Spanish Creole cottage once belonged to an Italian who immigrated to Florida as a soldier in the Spanish army. The unusual double-peaked roofline was created when the detached kitchen was

joined to the main house.

Dorr House
311 South Adams Street

The lifestyle of the merchant class in the late 1800s is shown in this restored Greek-revival residence furnished in the Victorian style. It was the home of Clara Barkley Dorr, widow of a partner in west Florida's largest lumber company.

Old Christ Church
405 South Adams Street

The earliest church in Florida still on its original site has been restored to its 1880s appearance. It is a favorite venue for weddings.

Lear-Rocheblave House
214 East Zaragoza Street

Built in 1890, this two-story late-Victorian home is furnished in the period of 1897 to 1913, when it was the residence of the family of Benito Rocheblave, a tug boat captain.

T. T. Wentworth, Jr., Florida State Museum
Address: 330 Jefferson Street
   Pensacola, FL 32502

Features: Children's Gallery, group tours
Admission: Free (school groups of more than ten should make reservations)
Phone: 850-595-5985
Website: www.historicpensacola. org

Once the Pensacola City Hall, this restored Italian Renaissance-style building houses the eclectic collection of T. T. Wentworth, Jr., as well as Civil War artifacts related to West Florida. Other highlights include artifacts from a 1559 shipwreck in Pensacola's harbor and printing press and documents related to the African American press in Pensacola. On the third floor, children can explore role-playing opportunities and hands-on experiences in the Children's Gallery.

Pensacola Historical Museum

Address: 115 East Zaragoza Street Pensacola, FL 32502
Features: Museum shop, research library
Hours: Monday-Saturday 10–4:30
Parking: Free
Phone: 850-433-1559
Website: www.pensacolahistory. org/museum.html

Interpretive exhibits highlighting Pensacola's past include early Native American artifact displays depicting events in military and maritime history, and stories of multi-ethnic groups that have contributed to the community's cultural variety. The museum, which is operated by the Pensacola Historical Society, is housed in the historic Arbona Building, built in the 1880s. The research library is located in the nearby Historical Resource Center at 110 East Church Street.

Pensacola Museum of Art

Address: 407 South Jefferson Street Pensacola, FL 32502
Features: Museum shop
Hours: Tuesday–Friday 10–5, Saturday & Sunday 12–4
Admission: Adults $5, students and military $2
Parking: Free
Phone: 850-432-6247
Website: www.pensacolamuseum ofart.org

Housed in the renovated 1908 city jail just south of the T. T. Wentworth Jr. Museum, this visual arts center emphasizes contemporary American art in its permanent collection of paintings and graphics and in the high caliber of its changing exhibits. The sturdy masonry building has an auditorium, classrooms and studios, and a reference library, in addition to its gallery space.

Pensacola Cultural Center

Address: 400 South Jefferson Street Pensacola, FL 32502
Phone: 850-434-0257
Website: www.pensacolalittle theatre.com

Across the street from the Pensacola Museum of Art is an exciting center for the performing arts, lodged in a renovated three-story building that once housed the

Escambia County Courthouse and the jail where public hangings were carried out until the 1920s. The 442-seat theater has state-of-the-art refinements that complement the performances of the Pensacola Little Theatre, and area dance and ballet companies. A fine restaurant is located in the Cultural Center atrium, which rises to the top of the building.

University of West Florida, Center for Fine and Performing Arts

Address: Building 82, 11000
   University Parkway
   Pensacola, FL 32514
Hours: Call for hours.
Admission: Gallery free
Parking: Free (use Parking Lot M)
Phone: 850-474-2541
Website: www.uwf.edu/cfpa

A stunning center for the arts—visual, musical, and dramatic—occupies a prime site on the main campus northwest of Pensacola. Enjoy Artist Series performances in the Music Hall and plays, opera, and symphonies in the 475-seat Mainstage Theater. The Art Gallery schedules changing shows of contemporary art and presents lectures, films, and videos to enhance the exhibits.

Pensacola Junior College, Anna Lamar Switzer Center for the Visual Arts

Address: 1000 College Boulevard
   Pensacola, FL 32504
Hours: Gallery Monday–Thursday
   8–9, Friday 8–3:30
Admission: Gallery free
Parking: Free

Phone: Gallery 850-484-2550
Website: www.pjc.
   edu/wisarts/gallery

This urban campus directs its cultural program toward the community as well as PJC students. In the galleries and hallways of the Center, built as a series of interlocking pods with flaring skylights, portions of the excellent permanent collection and temporary exhibits of international and national as well as student and faculty works are displayed.

National Museum of Naval Aviation

Address: 1750 Radford Boulevard
   Naval Air Station
   Pensacola, FL 32508
Features: Museum shop, café, re-
   search archives, art gallery,
   guided tours
Hours: Daily 9–5
Admission: Free, charge for
   IMAX® and flight simulator
Phone: 850-452-3604
Website: www.navalaviation
   museum.org

From the Navy's first wood-and-wire Triad to the sleek F/A-18 Hornet, more than 150 beautifully restored aircraft, scores of displays, and memorabilia detail naval aviation's rich history in

this handsome 300,000-square-foot facility. Walk the deck of a World War II aircraft carrier, visit a jungle air strip, or stroll down a 1943 street in the Home Front display. In the Pensacola-Blue Angels Atrium, a flight of Blue Angel Skyhawks hangs in the team's famous diamond formation. Guided tours of the museum are scheduled throughout the day, and die-hard airplane buffs will enjoy the bus tour of the restoration facility and flight line as well. For a real thrill, see *The Magic of Flight,* an exhilarating film experience in the IMAX® Theater, or take a ride in the motion-based flight simulator.

Fort Barrancas

Physical address: Naval Air
    Station, Pensacola
Mailing address: 1801 Gulf
    Breeze Parkway
    Gulf Breeze, FL 32561
Features: Book store, picnic area,
    nature trail, guided tours as
    posted
Hours: Daily 9:30–4:30
    (March–October), 8:30–3:45
    (November–February)
Admission: Free
Parking: Free
Phone: 850-934-2600
Website: www.nps.gov/guis

While at the Naval Air Station, visit this historic fort operated by the National Park Service as part of the Gulf Islands National Seashore. Many flags have flown from this strategic site opposite the entrance to Pensacola Harbor. The French occupied the site in 1719; the English built a naval fortification, which was captured by the Spanish in 1781 and enlarged; American forces under General Andrew Jackson seized the fort in 1814; the U.S. Navy built new defenses; and Confederate troops briefly held the fort in 1861. The extensive brick-lined, vaulted passageways and unique construction details of this fort remind the visitor of its importance as part of the nation's coastal defense. There is a small interpretive museum.

Fort Pickens

Physical address: Fort Pickens
    Road, Pensacola Beach, FL
Mailing address: 1801 Gulf Breeze
    Parkway
    Gulf Breeze, FL 32561
Features: Book store, camping,
    fishing, beach access, bicycle
    and nature trails, picnic area,
    guided tours as posted
Hours: Daily 8 a.m. to sunset
Admission: Per vehicle $8, per
    person on foot or bicycle $3
    (fee is good for 7 days)
NOTE: Due to hurricane damage,
    the Fort Pickens Road may be
    closed to auto traffic. Pedes-
    trians and cyclists are permitted
    on the seven-mile road, which,
    hopefully, will be repaired
    by 2009. Call for the latest
    information.

Phone: 850-934-2600
Website: www.nps.gov/guis

The largest of four forts built to protect Pensacola Bay and the Navy Yard stands on the western end of Santa Rosa Island. Here the remains of several nineteenth- and twentieth-century coastal fortifications survive—the earlier red brick fort contrasting with the massive concrete installations constructed later. Built with slave labor and used as a prison camp during the Civil War, the imposing old fort is the site of special candlelight tours. The Apache medicine man Geronimo, confined here in 1887 with his wives and followers, was the fort's most famous prisoner. Several frame buildings, former officer's and enlisted men's quarters, have been restored, and one functions as a museum of regional, natural, and cultural history and as an auditorium for films and lectures.

Naval Live Oaks Visitor Center

Address: 1801 Gulf Breeze
    Parkway
    Gulf Breeze, FL 32563
Features: Book shop, nature trails,
    picnic area
Hours: Park open daily 8 a.m. to
    sunset; Visitor center 8:30–4:30
Admission: Free

Parking: Free
Phone: 850-934-2600
Website: www.nps.gov/guis/

Shipbuilders in the nineteenth century prized the strong wood of the tough coastal live oak tree for frames and timbers, and the U.S. Navy set aside this grove of live oaks for its use in the nation's first tree farm in 1829. Exhibits show how the oak was harvested and shaped into the hulls of sturdy sailing vessels. This visitors' center in Gulf Breeze is the headquarters of the Gulf Islands National Seashore, a natural and historic resource preserve administered by the National Park Service and stretching 160 miles from Florida to Mississippi.

Fort Walton Beach

Beaches and water sports attract tourists and people stationed at nearby Eglin Air Force Base to this resort town on Florida's Emerald Coast.

Heritage Park and Cultural Center

Address: 139 Miracle Strip
    Parkway
    Fort Walton Beach, FL 32548
Features: Museum shop, research
    library
Hours: Monday–Saturday 10–4:30
    (August–May), Monday–Sat-
    urday 10–4:30, Sunday 12:00–
    4:30 (June–July)
Admission: Adults $5, seniors
    $4.50, children aged 6-17 $3,
    under age 6 free
Parking: Free
Phone: 850-833-9595

Visit three museums at this regional heritage site. The Indian Temple Mound Museum marks the site of an important political and ceremonial center for the Native Americans who inhabited this coast for centuries before Europeans landed. The museum, embellished with symbols drawn from the pre-Columbian pottery found in the area, is adjacent to a large mound topped with a replica of a temple built in the fifteenth century by the powerful Mississippi Culture. Imaginative exhibits of artifacts reflect the spiritual and artistic achievements of these early peoples. The Camp Walton Schoolhouse and the Garnier Post Office provide glimpses of early twentieth-century life in Fort Walton.

Air Force Armament Museum

Address: 100 Museum Drive
    Eglin Air Force Base, FL 32542
Features: Museum shop
Hours: Monday–Saturday
    9:30–4:30
Admission: Free
Parking: Free
Phone: 850-651-1808
Website: www.afarmament
    museum.com

Outside the west gate of Eglin Air Force Base on Highway 85 is a museum dedicated to the collection, preservation, and exhibition of airplanes, missiles, and other military hardware. Restored aircraft representing four wars can be seen inside the building, and others are on display outside. In addition, gun fanciers will find the modern and antique

weapons on exhibit in the vault of interest.

Valparaiso

This little town on a cove of Choctawhatchee Bay is off the beaten path, but it is a charming representative of the many rural communities in Florida that strive to preserve their special identity.

The Heritage Museum of Northwest Florida

Address: 115 Westview Avenue
    Valparaiso, FL 32580
Features: Museum shop, research
    library, classes
Hours: Tuesday–Saturday 10–4
Admission: Free
Parking: Free
Phone: 850-678-2615
Website: www.heritage-museum.
    org
E-mail: heritagemuseum@
    co.okaloosa.fl.us

This lively museum is housed in a former bank building in old Valparaiso. Graphic exhibits and displays of household implements, pioneer farming, and the local turpentine industry have the personal impact of an afternoon spent sitting in Grandma's kitchen or helping Grandpa with the chores.

Port Washington

Eden Gardens State Park

Address: 81 Eden Garden Road
    Port Washington, FL 32454
Features: Picnic area, guided tours
Hours: Gardens daily 8–sundown,
    house tours Thursday–Monday
    hourly 10–3

Admission: Per car $3; house tours
    adult $3, children $1.50
Parking: Free
Phone: 850-231-4214
Website: www.floridastateparks.
    org/edengardens

This tranquil site poised on a small
bayou about halfway between
Fort Walton and Panama City is
dominated by the gracious Wesley
house, built early in the twentieth
century as a family home and the
center of operations for William
Henry Wesley's busy lumber
enterprise. Lois Maxon, a later
owner, renovated the home in the
style of an antebellum plantation
mansion and furnished it with fine
antiques. Visitors will enjoy the
leisurely guided house tours, which
are held hourly Thursday through
Monday. The landscaped grounds
are open daily for picnicking
and strolling. In March, the peak
blooming season for azaleas
and camellias, the gardens are
particularly beautiful.

Panama City

Sparkling green waters and
white, sugar-sand beaches attract
thousands of visitors to Panama
City Beach every year. Historic
downtown Panama City deserves
a visit, too, for its interesting
collection of older buildings that
have been restored and converted
into shops, art galleries, and
restaurants.

Museum of Man in the Sea

Address: 17314 Panama City
    Beach Parkway
    Panama City Beach, FL 32413

Hours: Daily 10–4
Admission: Adults $5, children
    aged 6–16 $2.50
Parking: Free
Phone: 850-235-4101
E-mail: momits@bellsouth.net

Deep-sea diving has a longer
tradition than you might
think. This collection of diving
equipment, exhibits, and dioramas
focuses on the human fascination
with the underwater world—from
pearl and sponge divers, to
archaeologists and treasure hunters
who use sophisticated diving
equipment to explore sunken ships,
to those who dive for pleasure
and sport. Underwater research
vehicles such as the Navy's
Sealab are preserved here, as is
an extensive collection of diving
helmets and other military and
civilian underwater apparatus.

Junior Museum of Bay County

Address: 1731 Jenks Avenue
    Panama City, FL 32405
Hours: Monday–Friday 9–4:30,
    Saturday 10–4
Admission: $3 per person
Parking: Free
Phone: 850-769-6128
Website: www.jrmuseum.org

This hands-on museum will delight
every member of the family. The
young and the young at heart will
learn from the museum's science,
nature, and heritage experiences as
they explore Nature Play, Imagine
Me, and Toddler Town, and as
they visit the restored pioneer
homestead and stroll on the nature
trail.

Visual Art Center of Northwest Florida

Address: 19 East Fourth Street
Panama City, FL 32401
Features: Museum shop, classes, lectures
Hours: Monday, Wednesday, Friday 10–4, Tuesday, Thursday 10–8, Saturday 1–5
Admission: Free
Parking: Free
Phone: 850-769-4451

The 1920s City Hall has been restored and adapted into a spacious art center in the heart of old Panama City. The main gallery in the center, where continuously changing exhibits are on view, is a terrific art space—light, airy, and inviting. There are two smaller galleries on the first floor and studios for class and individual work on the upper level of the center. The Art Academy provides challenging art instruction for school children at all grade levels, and art appreciation lectures keyed to the current exhibit are hosted for the general public.

Port St. Joe

In the 1830s, an early group of promoters proposed an ambitious series of canals and railroads to link this sheltered harbor to Pensacola and Apalachicola. When these territorial development projects failed, the port went into decline. Today, St. Joseph's State Park and Cape San Blas National Wildlife Refuge attract visitors to the area.

Constitutional Convention Museum State Park

Address: 200 Allen Memorial Way
Port St. Joe, FL 32456
Hours: Thursday–Monday 9–12 and 1–5
Admission: $1, under age 6 free
Parking: Free
Phone: 850-229-8029
Website: www.floridastateparks.org/constitutionconvention

Florida's first constitution was written by delegates to the territorial convention that met here in 1838 and 1839. An imposing monument set within a park commemorates this event. Although Florida's application to join the United States was immediately forwarded to Congress, statehood was not granted until 1845. Documents and artifacts that help put these early events in Florida's history in perspective are on display in the museum, which also features an animated diorama and biographies of the elected delegates.

Apalachicola

Stroll around this once-thriving cotton port at the mouth of the Apalachicola River, and take time to admire the lovely churches, burial grounds, cotton warehouses, stores, and homes that evoke memories of the plantation era. The restored Gibson Inn in the center of town still provides hospitality to travelers, and the 1830s Raney House on Market Street is open for tours on Saturday afternoons. The annual seafood festival held each November celebrates the twentieth-century focus of Apalachicola's economy.

John Gorrie Museum State Park

Address: 46 Sixth Street
    Apalachicola, FL 32329
Hours: Thursday–Monday 9–5
Admission: $1, under age 6 free
Parking: Free
Phone: 850-653-9347
Website: www.floridastateparks.
    org/johngorriemuseum

Dr. John Gorrie invented a machine to make artificial ice in the 1840s as part of the treatment for his yellow fever and malaria patients. His invention became a forerunner of modern refrigeration and air conditioning equipment, and he received the first U.S. patent for mechanical refrigeration in 1851. The state of Florida considered Dr. Gorrie's invention so significant that it honored him by placing his statue in Statuary Hall in the U.S. Capitol. This small museum has a model of his remarkable ice machine, as well as displays showing what life was like in the town's heyday as a prosperous pre-Civil War cotton port.

Bristol

Gregory Mansion, Torreya State Park

Address: 2576 NW Torreya Park
    Road
    Bristol, FL 32321
Features: Guided house tours,
    picnic area, nature trails,
    camping
Hours: Daily, 8–sunset, house
    tours on weekdays at 10, on

weekends and holidays at 10, 2, and 4
Admission: Park, $2 per car; house tours, adults $2, under age 13 $1
Parking: Free
Phone: 850-643-2674
Website: www.floridastateparks.
    org/torreya

The determined and resourceful traveler who seeks out this park will discover not only a stunning scenic area reminiscent of the Appalachian Mountains, but also the magnificent pre-Civil War Gregory Mansion overlooking the Apalachicola River. This state park was developed by the Civilian Conservation Corps in the 1930s. The men of the CCC moved the mansion, built in 1849, from its endangered site across the river to the high bluff where it now stands, fully furnished with period antiques. This antebellum plantation house is one of the few to survive, and its dramatic history is admirably interpreted during guided tours. Note that hours of the house tours are limited and that the park is in the Eastern Time zone.

St. Marks

Now a small fishing village, this was an important cotton port when a railroad was extended from Tallahassee in the 1830s. The railroad bed has been paved and converted to recreational use as the sixteen-mile Tallahassee-St. Marks Historic Trail, popular with hikers, horseback riders, skaters, and cyclists.

San Marcos de Apalache Historic State Park

Address: 148 Old Fort Road
   St. Marks, FL 32355
Features: Museum shop, picnic
   area, nature trail
Hours: Thursday–Monday 9–5
Admission: $1.00, under age 6 free
Parking: Free
Phone: 850-925-6216
Website: www.floridastateparks.
   org/sanmarcos

Several forts were established at various times on this point of land because of its strategic location at the mouth of the St. Marks and Wakulla Rivers. Only earthworks and limestone and brick foundations remain, but the history of the site is interpreted in the museum, constructed on the foundation of a hospital built before the Civil War. A vivid cast of characters has played on this stage: the men of De Soto's expedition, pirates and Native Americans, soldiers of Spain and England, adventurers and traders, U.S. troops, Confederate and Union forces. An informative self-guided brochure is a welcome aid to a tour of the grounds. The Tallahassee-St. Marks Trail ends at the historic site, where an additional treat may await you: manatees can often be seen from the banks of the Wakulla River.

Tallahassee

Florida's capital city spreads like an intricately patterned coverlet over seven gentle hills. Oak-canopied roads and antebellum architectural gems emphasize the city's Old South charm, while governmental centers and two state universities focus on the New South's progress. This site was chosen as the state capital in the early 1800s because it was halfway between St. Augustine and Pensacola, Florida's population centers at the time.

The Historic Old Capitol

Address: 402 South Monroe Street
   Tallahassee, FL 32399
Hours: Monday–Friday 9–4:30,
   Saturday 10:00–4:30, Sunday
   12:00–4:30
Admission: Free
Parking: At Kleman Plaza Garage
Phone: 850-487-1902

Bold red-and-white-striped awnings on the restored 1902 capitol strike an inviting note that welcomes visitors to this museum of Florida's governmental history. The legislative chambers, state supreme court, and governor's office have been restored to their turn-of-the-nineteenth-century appearance, and lively exhibits document the colorful events of Florida's political past. Notice the careful restoration of the colored glass in the dome, and walk down the broad central stairway to see the changing exhibits in the basement gallery.

The New Capitol and the Capitol Gallery

Address: 400 South Monroe Street
    Tallahassee, FL 32399
Hours: Monday-Friday 8–5
Admission: Free
Phone: 850-488-6167 (Capitol
    Welcome Center)

Across the courtyard from the Historic Old Capitol, check out the information desk inside the west entrance of the New Capitol, a gleaming modern skyscraper. In the hallways, notice historic photographs and the work of contemporary Florida artists. Visitors are invited to observe when the legislature is in session. Take the elevator to the twenty-second floor for a panoramic view of Tallahassee and a visit to the Capitol Gallery, which features changing exhibits of the works of distinguished Florida artists.

Union Bank Black Archives

Address: 219 Apalachee Parkway
    Tallahassee, FL 32399
Hours: Monday–Friday 9–4
Admission: Free
Parking: Metered parking
Phone: 850-561-2603

Artifacts and documents celebrating Florida's rich African-American heritage are displayed in this small building across from the Old Capital. Florida's oldest surviving bank building, constructed by slave labor in 1841, served as a bank for plantation owners during Florida's territorial period. After the Civil War, it became a Freedman's Bureau bank for newly-emancipated African Americans. It was moved to its present site in 1971 and is now an extension of the Black Archives Research Center and Museum located on the FAMU campus.

Mary Brogan Museum of Art and Science

Address: 350 South Duval Street
    Tallahassee, FL 32301
Hours: Monday–Saturday 10–5
Admission: Adults $6, seniors, students and military $3.50
Parking: At Kleman Plaza Garage
Phone: 850-513-0700
Website: www.thebrogan.org

In one modern building located on the Kleman Plaza in downtown Tallahassee, MOAS visitors will find two distinctive museum experiences. The elegant art museum is the place for art and music events, and the interactive science museum will engage young minds and involve families in scientific discovery, especially during special programs on Saturday.

Museum of Florida History

Address: 500 South Bronough
    Street
    Tallahassee, FL 32399
Hours: Monday–Friday 9–4:30,
    Saturday 10–4:30, Sunday
    12–4:30
Admission: Free
Parking: Visitor parking in adjacent garage
Phone: 850-245-6400
Website: www.museumofflorida
    history.com

Florida history is preserved, exhibited, and interpreted in intriguing displays of mastodon bones, Native American pottery, sunken Spanish treasure, a reconstructed river steamer, a 1920s Tin-Can Tourist camper rig, a 1930s citrus-packing house, and other displays that bring history to life. Many of the exhibits assembled here will travel throughout Florida, documenting exciting facets of the state's history. Enjoy your time-travel in Florida's official history museum, located on the lower level of the R. A. Gray Building, which also houses the state archives.

been restored to its 1928 period when the Knott family, prominent in state politics, moved in. Mrs. Luella Knott tied her whimsical poems to many of the home's Victorian-era furnishings, to the delight of both her guests and today's visitors who are welcomed to this friendly and charming house museum.

Brokaw-McDougall House

Address: 329 North Meridian
　　Street
　　Tallahassee, FL 32301
Hours: Monday–Friday 9–5
Admission: Free
Parking: Free
Phone: 850-891-3900
Website: www.talgov.com

The Knott House Museum

Address: 301 East Park Avenue
　　Tallahassee, FL 32301
Hours: Wednesday–Friday 1–4,
　　Saturday 10–4; guided tours on
　　the hour
Admission: Free
Parking: Metered spaces
Phone: 850-922-2459
Website: www.museumofflorida
　　history.com

Known as "the house that rhymes," this time capsule of Tallahassee history is in the heart of the Park Avenue historic district. The antebellum mansion has

One of the finest remaining antebellum homes in Tallahassee was built around 1856 by a prosperous livery stable owner who also served in the state legislature. The strikingly fashionable residence remained in the same family until the 1970s, when the classical-revival mansion with its stately live oak trees and formal gardens became the headquarters of the Historic Tallahassee Preservation Board. It is currently managed by the city of Tallahassee.

LeMoyne Center for the Visual Arts

Address: 125 North
Gadsden Street
Tallahassee, FL 32301
Features: Museum shop, lectures,
classes
Hours: Tuesday–Saturday 10–5,
Sunday 1–5
Admission: Adults $2 donation,
free on Sunday
Parking: Free
Phone: 850-222-8800
Website: www.lemoyne.org
E-mail: art@lemoyne.org

Located in a complex of buildings
in Tallahassee's Park Avenue
historic district, the LeMoyne
has been the city's art center for
nearly fifty years. It is named for
Jacques LeMoyne de Morgues, the
first artist known to have visited
the New World as a member
of a sixteenth-century French
expedition to Florida. Works from
the permanent collection of Florida
artists alternate with stimulating
and innovative contemporary
shows in the galleries, while
the education wing hums with
the excitement and intensity of
art classes and workshops. The
gracefully landscaped sculpture
garden in the rear is a popular
place for weddings and special
events.

Riley House Museum of African-American History and Culture

Address: 419 East Jefferson Street
Tallahassee, FL 32311
Hours: Monday–Friday 10–4
Admission: Adults $1, children $2
Parking: Free
Phone: 850-681-7881
Website: www.rileymuseum.org

This attractively restored two-story house museum located a
few blocks east of the Florida
capitol was once the home of
John G. Riley, a freed slave who
became a leader in the business
community and served for thirty-three years as the principal of
Lincoln High School, built to
provide education for newly freed
slaves in Tallahassee. Exhibits and
furnishings in the 1890s home,
which was the center of a small,
middle-class, African-American
neighborhood, are related to the
ancestry and history of the African
Americans in Florida. The Riley
House is also the headquarters
of the Florida African American
Heritage Preservation Network.

Goodwood Museum and Gardens

Address: 1600 Miccosukee Road
Tallahassee, FL 32308
Hours: House tours are Monday–
Friday 10–4, Saturday 10–2
Garden hours: Monday–Friday 9–
5, Saturday 10–2
Admission: House tours $5, under
age 3 free; admission to garden
is free
Parking: Free
Phone: 850-877-4202
Website: www.goodwoodmuseum.
org

The history of Goodwood
Plantation is a history of Florida: a

number of prominent owners have made significant contributions to the state's social and political history. This sixteen-acre Tallahassee showplace includes a magnificently restored 1840s mansion, sixteen out-buildings, a roller rink, and a reflecting pool. The grounds are shaded by centuries-old live oak trees and adorned with old varieties of roses and heirloom plantings that reflect gardens that bloomed in the early 1900s.

Florida State University, Museum of Fine Arts, Mainstage Theater, and Ruby Diamond Auditorium

Address: Fine Arts Building, 530 Call Street
Tallahassee, FL 32306
Museum Hours: Monday–Friday 9–4, Saturday and Sunday 1–4 (closed weekends in summer)
Admission: Free
Parking: Metered visitor spaces in parking garage at Tennessee and Macomb Streets
Phone: Museum 850-644-6836

Visual and performing arts are on view in the Fine Arts Building, a modern red-brick complex located on the northern edge of the main campus. Here, academic and professional training for students is enhanced by the regular appearance of outstanding guest artists. The museum is a major art exhibition space with permanent collections of pre-Columbian, Eastern, European, and contemporary American works. Changing events include one-person shows and thematic exhibits of exceptional quality. The Mainstage Theater is the premier showcase for major productions by FSU's acclaimed School of Theater. Ruby Diamond Auditorium, located in Westcott Hall at the main entrance to the university, is an elegant venue for performances of the University Symphony Orchestra and the Florida State Opera.

Florida Agricultural and Mechanical University, Fine Arts Gallery and Black Archives

Address: FAMU, Tallahassee, FL 32314
Hours: Monday–Friday 9–5, closed 12–1
Admission: Free
Parking: Pick up campus map, directions, and visitor parking sticker at Parking Services at the corner of Wahnish Way and Gamble Street
Phone: Fine Arts Gallery 850-599-3161, Black Archives 850-599-3020

Located on the attractive, hilly FAMU campus just south of downtown Tallahassee, the Fine Arts Gallery in the Foster-Tanner Building is well worth a visit. The white-columned Carnegie Center, originally a library and the oldest building on campus, is the home of the Florida Black Archives, where visually exciting displays of artifacts depict African-American life and culture.

Tallahassee Museum

Address: 3945 Museum Drive
Tallahassee, FL 32310

Features: Museum shop, café, classes
Hours: Monday–Saturday 9–5, Sunday 12:30–5 (nature trail closes daily at 4:50)
Admission: Adults $9, seniors $8.50, children $6, under age 4 free
Parking: Free
Phone: 850-576-1636
Website: www.tallahasseemuseum.org

This marvelous fifty-two-acre outdoor museum features live animals native to Florida in their natural habitats, a changing exhibits gallery, a hands-on Discovery Center, nature trails, and an evocative collection of historic buildings, including an antebellum plantation house once owned by a princess, an African-American church and school, and a nineteenth-century Cracker farmstead.

Alfred B. Maclay Gardens State Park

Address: 3540 Thomasville Road
Tallahassee, FL 32309
Features: Gardening classes, picnic area, boating, fishing, nature trails
Hours: Daily 8–sundown
Admission: Park $4 per vehicle; gardens adults $4, children $2
Parking: Free
Phone: 850-487-4115
Website: www.floridastatepark.org/maclay

This picturesque, lakeside garden of native and exotic plants is particularly vivid in the peak season from January through April. Visit the charming Maclay house (open only during peak season) and learn more about the New York sportsman who developed this horticultural jewel on his southern estate in the 1920s. Take a leisurely stroll along scenic pathways, through the Secret Garden, and past the reflecting pool to Lake Hall. You may also enjoy boating, fishing, swimming, and picnicking in this 308-acre, state-owned park, as well as exploring the hiking and cycling trails in the adjacent 877-acre Lake Overstreet Addition Recreation Area.

Lake Jackson Mounds Archaeological State Park

Address: 3600 Indian Mound Road
Tallahassee, FL 32308
Features: Picnic area, nature trails
Hours: Daily 8–sundown
Admission: $2 per vehicle
Parking: Free
Phone: 850-922-6007
Website: www.floridastateparks.org

This significant state archaeological site sheds light on the way of life of the agrarian moundbuilders who lived in this area between 1300 and 1500 A.D. A number of earthen ceremonial mounds can still be seen on the wooded site north of the city near Lake Jackson. A meandering nature trail through hardwood ravines and upland pinewoods leads to the site of an early eighteenth-century grist mill.

41

Mission San Luis de Apalachee

Address: 2021 West Mission Road
Tallahassee, FL 32304
Features: Museum shop, guided
tours, costumed interpreters,
picnic area
Hours: Tuesday–Sunday 10–4
Admission: Free
Parking: Free
Phone: 850-487-3711

Spread over a glorious fifty-
acre hilltop area is the active
archaeological site of a
seventeenth-century Apalachee
Indian village and Spanish mission.
View the orientation video in
the visitors' center to place this
important early colonial site in
perspective, then follow the well-
marked trails around the extensive
grounds. Based on archaeological
and historical research, buildings
and features such as a Spanish
house, the plaza, the Franciscan
mission church, the Apalachee
council house, and the fort have
been reconstructed. Visitors can
engage in an ongoing dialogue
with the past, thanks to the
"residents," costumed interpreters
who take on the personas of those
who once lived here.

Tallahassee Antique Car Museum

Address: 6800 Mahan Drive
Tallahassee, FL 32308

Features: Museum shop
Hours: Monday–Saturday 10–5,
Sunday 12–5
Admission: Adults $7.50, children
aged 11–15 $5, under age 11
$4
Parking: Free
Phone: 850-942-0137
Website: www.tacm.com

America's love affair with the
automobile is celebrated in this
collection of rare antique cars,
each in running order and pristine
condition. From the 1903 Stanley
Steamer to the 1997 Plymouth
Prowler, more than fifty vehicles
and related auto memorabilia
are displayed. Also on exhibit is
an 1884 Duryea, believed to the
oldest American auto.

Perry

A major industry since the 1800s,
forestry is still the most vital
aspect of this north Florida town's
economy. Each October thousands
of visitors attend the Florida
Forest Festival to celebrate the
remarkable diversity and enduring
importance of the state's timber
industry.

Forest Capital Museum State Park

Address: 204 Forest Park Drive
Perry, FL 32348
Features: Picnic area, playground
Hours: Thursday–Monday 9–12,
1–5
Admission: $1, under age 6 free
Parking: Free
Phone: 850-584-3227
Website: www.floridastateparks.
org/forestcapital

More than three hundred

different species of trees grow within Florida's boundaries. This museum, located sixty miles southeast of Tallahassee, displays a unique map of Florida using sixty-one of these trees in its stately design. Permanent displays in the circular exhibit hall focus on Florida's forest industry. Included is a talking tree, designed to delight and inform young children. An 1863 Cracker homestead adjacent to the museum depicts the self-sufficient life of the pioneers who built their homes in the piney woods. The distinctive architecture of these early settlers, who relied on the abundance of pine trees in the area, is reflected in the cabin and in typical farm buildings such as the smoke house, corn crib, and log barn.

Madison

Madison and its environs abound in natural beauty and historic treasures. Many of the buildings in the downtown area around the handsome courthouse have been restored and renovated, and the Four Freedoms Park with its large gazebo is the scene of band concerts and festive celebrations. Madison is also the home of North Florida Community College, founded in the 1950s.

The Treasures of Madison County

Address: 214 Southwest Range
    Avenue
    Madison, FL 32340
Hours: Monday–Friday 10–2,
    Saturday 10–12
Admission: Free
Parking: Free

Phone: 850-973-3661
Website: www.madisonfla.com

The WT Davis building has taken on a new life as the historical museum of Madison County. Fresh and varied exhibits are offered three or four times a year, with subjects ranging from art, Americana, and antique toys to memorabilia and artifacts documenting daily life and the passage of time in this north Florida community.

Live Oak

The southern live oak tree is the symbol of the county seat of Suwannee County, which has retained its engaging Southern charm and hospitality. Explore the historic downtown and surrounding residential neighborhoods, and admire the landmark county courthouse in the center of Live Oak.

Suwannee County Historical Museum

Address: 208 North Ohio Avenue
    Live Oak, FL 32064
Features: Museum shop
Hours: Monday–Friday, 9–3
Admission: Donation
Parking: Free
Phone: 904-362-1776
E-mail: suwanneemuseum@yahoo.
    com

The sturdy brick freight station, once a busy center of commercial activity when Atlantic Coast Line trains pulled into and out of Live Oak regularly, is now a cultural center for the community.

In addition to displays of Native American artifacts, antique vehicles, pioneer crafts, family treasures, and a wonderful copper moonshine still, visitors to the museum will catch glimpses of everyday life in times past in the thematic exhibits.

Jasper

Hamilton County Old Jail Historical Museum

Address: 501 Northeast First
    Avenue
    Jasper FL 32052
Hours: Monday–Friday 10–3
Admission: Free
Parking: Free
Phone: 386-792-3050
Website: http://www.rootsweb.
    com/~flhchms/
E-mail: oldjailmuseum@alltell.net

This red-brick jail, built in 1893 in Jasper, the county seat of Hamilton County, is completely intact, including a hanging tower in front and the original steel-and-

concrete cells on the second floor. The sheriff's family lived on the first floor, and the kitchen where the sheriff's wife prepared meals on a wood stove for the prisoners has been recreated. The old jail serves now as the county historical museum.

White Springs

"Way Down Upon the Suwannee River" is the theme song of one of Florida's oldest tourist resorts, still a delightful place to visit. It is now a historic district listed on the National Register of Historic Places. The medicinal qualities of the mineral springs once drew health seekers by the hundreds to fill the dozen or so hotels and boarding houses. Today the river, the town, and the forests attract canoeists, hikers, and cyclists in even greater numbers.

Stephen Foster State Folk Culture Center

Address: P.O. Drawer G
    White Springs, FL 32096
Features: Picnic area, nature trails,
    bicycle trails, camping, canoe
    launch, craft shop
Hours: Daily 8–sundown, build-
    ings open 9–5
Admission: $4 per vehicle (up to 8
    passengers)
Phone: 386-397-2733
Website: www.floridastateparks.
    org/stephenfoster

Dedicated to nineteenth-century composer Stephen Foster, who never saw the Suwannee River he romanticized in his song, this state park features a restored carillon tower that plays Foster's music and a museum in an antebellum-style mansion with dioramas and exhibits related to his songs and his life. Also on the grounds, on the banks of the Suwannee River, is the replica of the Spring House that drew many tourists to the resort area at the turn of the nineteenth century. As the hub of Florida folk culture today, the center offers festivals and events throughout the year, workshops and demonstrations in the Craft Square, music and dance, storytelling, and rural folkways unique to Florida. The Florida Folk Festival, held each Memorial Day weekend, draws the best of the state's folk performers and artisans to delight large and enthusiastic crowds.

early 1868 and left a vivid record of his observations. The charming little fishing village has attracted artists, writers, naturalists, and connoisseurs of spectacular sunsets. Crowds swell the local population twice a year for the annual Seafood Festival and Arts Festival.

Cedar Key Historical Society Museum

Address: P.O. Box 222
   Cedar Key, FL 32625
Hours: Sunday–Friday 1–4,
   Saturday 11–5
Admission: Adults $1, children
   $.50
Parking: Free
Phone: 352-543-5549
Website: www.cedarkeymuseum.
   org
E-mail: cedarcedar@bellsouth.net

This downtown museum is housed in one of Cedar Key's venerable storefront buildings. The collection of photographs, period clothing, tools and equipment, and Native American artifacts gives visitors a taste of the richness and diversity of life in the Gulf coast community. The Andrews House, built in 1909, has been moved next to the museum, greatly expanding its display and archival storage space.

Cedar Key

John Muir, noted naturalist and conservation pioneer, spent several months in Cedar Key in 1867 and

You may purchase a walking tour booklet here and enjoy learning about the history of Cedar Key as you stroll around the island.

Cedar Key Museum State Park

Address: 12231 Southwest
    166 Court
    Cedar Key, FL 32625
Features: Museum shop
Hours: Thursday–Monday 9–5
Admission: Adults $1, under age
    6 free
Parking: Free
Phone: 352-543-5350
Website: www.floridastateparks.
    org/cedarkeymuseum

The area's colorful past is depicted in this comprehensive museum located two miles northwest of town. Prehistoric artifacts collected in shell middens and underwater sites reveal the longtime presence of humans on this coast. Other interpretive displays touch on the role of the Seahorse Key Lighthouse in the Seminole Wars, the pre-Civil War railroad that linked Cedar Key to the Atlantic Coast, the blockade runners of the Civil War era, and the lumber industry boom that stripped the islands of cedar trees to create millions of pencils. Also of interest is the fine shell collection assembled by St. Clair Whitman, a longtime resident of Cedar Key. Whitman's shingled vernacular-style island home has been moved to the museum grounds and restored.

2.

Northeast Florida

Jacksonville

Lake City

St. Augustine

Gainesville

Fernandina Beach

This historic seaport on Amelia Island has a fascinating past that can be sensed today in its restored downtown Centre Street and nearby residential districts. Elegant neighborhoods invite visitors to stroll and admire the architectural diversity and quality of the historic buildings. Fernandina was a wealthy, bustling cotton-shipping port before the Civil War, linked to Cedar Key on the Gulf coast by one of Florida's first railroads. Begin your coastal journey on the Buccaneer Trail from this revitalized First Coast resort town.

Amelia Island Museum of History

Address: 233 S. 3rd Street
    Fernandina Beach, FL 32034
Features: Research library, lectures, guided walking and driving tours for groups
Hours: Monday–Saturday 10–4, Sunday 1–4; walk-in museum tours at 11 and 2 Admission: Museum tours, adults $7, students and military $4
Parking: Free
Phone: 904-261-7378
Website: www.ameliamuseum.org
E-mail: info@ameliamuseum.org

Eight flags have flown over Florida's northernmost seaport. All are represented, as are prehistoric cultures, in this dynamic spoken-history museum located a few

blocks south of historic Centre Street. Eloquent interpreters guide visitors through four thousand years of Amelia Island history and the saga of the eight flags. Once the Nassau County jailhouse, this award-winning museum, whose mission is to combine pleasure with education, has an excellent library and archives collection. Visitors who take walking and driving tours of Amelia Island's historic districts led by the museum docents are also in for a lively chronicle of the ups and downs of this deep-water seaport and antebellum railroad center, Florida's earliest posh oceanfront resort.

Fort Clinch State Park

Address: 2601 Atlantic Avenue
    Fernandina Beach, FL 32034
Features: Museum shop, nature
    trails, picnic area, beaches,
    fishing pier, campsites
Hours: Daily, park: 8–sundown;
    fort 9–5
Admission: $5 per vehicle (up to 8
    passengers), $1 extra per person
    to visit the fort
Phone: 904-277-7274
Website: www.floridastateparks.
    org/fortclinch

Florida Park Service rangers, uniformed as Federal soldiers of the Civil War period, go about their daily chores and chat with visitors as they recreate life in the 1860s in this garrison on Cumberland Sound. The restored fortress features splendid

brickwork, cannons on the ramparts, military quarters, a stunning natural setting overlooking Cumberland Island, and a small interpretive museum explaining the history of the fort. Although it holds only a minor place in Florida's military history and was never the scene of bombardment or siege, it is a reminder of the importance coastal forts once held in national defense. Fort Clinch State Park was one of Florida's first state parks, developed as a recreational/historical resource by the Civilian Conservation Corps (CCC) in the 1930s. A three-mile canopied road winds through dense woodland, and other natural advantages can be enjoyed: walking and bicycling trails, fishing, and picnicking.

Fort George Island

This historic island south of Fernandina Beach is heavily wooded and has an ageless, timeless quality.

Kingsley Plantation

Address: 11676 Palmetto Avenue
   Jacksonville, FL 32226
Features: Museum shop, ranger
   programs
Hours: Daily 9–5
Admission: Free
Parking: Free
Phone: 904-251-3537
Website: www.nps.gov/timu

This restored plantation, one of the oldest in Florida, links the Spanish, English, and American occupations of the island and interprets the lives and work of the people, free and enslaved, who lived in north Florida during its plantation era. Remains of twenty-five slave quarters built of tabby, a primitive oyster shell concrete, and kitchen, house, and barn merit a leisurely visit. The eighteenth-century house faces the Fort George River and a quiet anchorage. Kingsley Plantation is now part of the extensive Timucuan Ecological and Historic Preserve.

Jacksonville Beach

Once called Pablo Beach, this oceanfront community is part of Florida's First Coast. Miles of wide, white-sand beaches attract visitors for sunning, swimming, shelling, and surfing.

Beaches Museum and History Center

Address: 380 Pablo Avenue
   Jacksonville Beach, FL 32250
Features: Guided tours, archives,
   outdoor exhibit
Hours: Tuesday–Saturday, 10–4:30
Admission: Adults $5, seniors $4,
   children aged 6–17 $3
Phone: 904-241-5657
Website: www.beachesarea
   historicalsociety.com
E-mail: BAHS1978@aol.com

The Museum and History Center, featuring changing exhibits, is located on Pablo Avenue, but the outdoor exhibit is at 425 Beach Boulevard. There you will find an antique railroad engine and historic buildings set within an attractive park, reminders of the good old days when tourists arrived at Florida's famous beach resorts by train. This outdoor exhibit celebrates the history of Mayport, Atlantic Beach, Neptune Beach, Jacksonville Beach, Ponte Vedra Beach, and Palm Valley. Tours of the railroad foreman's home and of the depot, painted yellow with white trim (a color scheme favored by railroad builder Henry Flagler for many of his Florida East Coast railroad buildings) will introduce visitors to those who made a good living "workin' on the railroad."

Jacksonville

A cosmopolitan city, Jacksonville enjoys a year-round banquet of art events and theatrical and musical series. Handsome historic districts and major museums add to the flavor of this city built on the sweeping curve of the St. Johns River. Take time to stroll along the riverfront boardwalks and savor some of the many outdoor festivals, ranging from jazz fests to ethnic carnivals.

Fort Caroline

Address: 12713 Fort Caroline
     Road
     Jacksonville, FL 32225
Features: Picnic area, nature trails
Hours: Daily 9–5
Admission: Free
Parking: Free
Phone: 904-641-7155
Website: www.nps.gov/foca

A monument and a reconstructed fort on the banks of the St. Johns River mark the existence of the French colonists who laid claim to this area in1564. Within a few years this settlement was destroyed by Spanish forces sent up from newly established St. Augustine, thus ending the French colonial presence in Florida. The National Park Service operates this site, which is a national memorial, and the associated museum, which eloquently interprets the first confrontation between European powers in the New World. Fort Caroline is now part of the Timucuan Ecological and Historic Preserve, named for the Native Americans who once inhabited this fertile coastal region.

University of North Florida, Art Gallery

Address: Founders Hall/ Building
     2 4567 St. Johns Bluff Road
     Jacksonville, FL 32224
Hours: Monday, Wednesday,
     Thursday 9–5, Tuesday 9–7,
     Friday 9–3
Admission: Free
Parking: Campus parking fee $3
Phone: 904-620-2534
Website: www.unf.edu/dept/gallery

The University Gallery plays an integral role in the cultural offerings of UNF and the surrounding metropolitan area. The exhibition schedule features individual and group exhibitions by artists of regional and national renown and group shows featuring UNF art faculty and art majors. Additional offerings include lectures, musical performances, poetry readings and films.

Florida Community College at Jacksonville, South Gallery and Wilson Center for the Arts

Address: 11901 Beach Boulevard
     Jacksonville, FL 32246
Hours: Gallery Monday,
     Wednesday, Friday 10–4;
     Thursday 10–7
Admission: Free
Parking: Free
Phone: Gallery 904-646-2023, box
     office 904-646-2222
Website: www.fccj.edu/campuses/
     south/wilson/south_gallery.
     html

Overlooking a serene lake, the Nathan H. Wilson Center for the Arts features a dazzling theater space on the FCCJ South Campus. The spacious main lobby of the building is set off by wrought-iron railings designed to look like tall, graceful sea grasses. The main stage and a smaller studio theater with the latest and best technical facilities host a varied and sophisticated artists' series. South Gallery, a well-lighted, wedge-shaped display space adjacent to the lobby, shows the works of regional and international artists.

Jacksonville University, Alexander Brest Museum and Gallery, Swisher Auditorium, and Terry Concert Hall

Address: 2800 University Boulevard North Jacksonville, FL 32211
Hours: Museum Monday–Friday 9–4:30
Admission: Free
Parking: Free
Phone: Gallery 904-256-7374
Website: http://arts.ju.edu/art/gallery.html

The JU campus, nestled under a canopy of oaks and embellished with outdoor sculpture by major American artists, overlooks the St. Johns River. The collection at the Alexander Brest Museum contains a large group of Oriental and European ivories, nineteenth- and twentieth-century glass, Mesoamerican artifacts, and twentieth-century porcelain. Monthly exhibits of regional and internationally known artists are also featured. Theatrical and

musical performances are among the regular offerings at the Swisher Auditorium and the Terry Concert Hall, located adjacent to the museum.

Jacksonville Museum of Contemporary Art

Address: 333 N Laura Street Jacksonville, FL 32202
Features: Museum shop, café, art walks, film series
Hours: Tuesday, Thursday, Friday, Saturday, Sunday 10–4, Wednesday 10–9
Admission: General $6, students and seniors $4, under age 2 free
Parking: Nearby parking garage or on-street metered parking
Phone: 904-366-6911
Website: www.mocajacksonville.org

This fine art museum is fitted into a historic brick warehouse in downtown Jacksonville, but the vibrantly fashioned interior shimmers with cutting-edge art works exhibited on several levels. A special space for young art lovers is tucked into the top floor.

Museum of Science and History

Address: 1025 Museum Circle Jacksonville, FL 32207
Features: Museum shop
Hours: Monday–Friday 10–5, Saturday 10–6, Sunday 1–6
Admission: Adults $9, seniors $7.50, children aged 3–12 $7
Parking: Free
Phone: 904-396-6674
Website: www.themosh.org

The emphasis at the MOSH is on

hands-on activities, interactive programs, and stimulating educational exhibits. The ground floor is devoted to the natural sciences. Enter the world of the great sea mammals—the whales, dolphins, and manatees; visit the Florida Naturalists' Center, stocked with live critters; and refresh your senses in the wetlands environment of the Hixon Courtyard. On the second floor, get caught up in the "Currents of Time" historical exhibit as you walk through twelve thousand years that chronicle northeast Florida's rich cultural heritage with the imaginative use of vivid murals, authentic artifacts, special effects, historic photographs, and period costumes and furnishings. Experience science "outside the box" in the Universe of Science. Also featured are KidSpace for the very young, a planetarium, and a science theater, as well as changing exhibits that will delight young and not-so-young visitors to this museum located in the city's riverfront district.

Jacksonville Maritime Museum

Address: 1015 Museum Circle, Unit 2
Jacksonville, FL 32207
Hours: Monday–Friday 10:30–3, Saturday and Sunday 1–5
Admission: Free
Parking: Free
Phone: 904-398-9011

Welcome aboard this museum on the south bank of the St. Johns River. The museum preserves and celebrates the city's rich maritime heritage, which began in the 1560s when French colonists at Fort Caroline built two vessels of native wood. Surrounded by artifacts, memorabilia, scale models, and photographs, and aided by the enthusiastic interpretations of volunteer docents, visitors depart with a richer understanding of the area's seafaring past and present. And if you are fascinated by the story of the *Titanic,* ask to see this exhibit and learn the facts behind the myths that surround this marine tragedy.

Karpeles Manuscript Library

Address: 101 West First Street
Jacksonville, FL 32206
Hours: Tuesday–Saturday 10–4, Sunday 12–4
Admission: Free
Parking: Free on-street parking
Phone: 904-356-2992
Website: http://www.rain.org/
~karpeles/jaxfrm.html

One of seven manuscript libraries established by David Karpeles throughout the country is housed in Jacksonville's historic Christian Science church building in Springside. Within this 1921 neoclassical landmark are changing

exhibits of original manuscripts, drafts, letters, handwritten documents, and musical scores from the vast collection of manuscripts preserved by Karpeles. Additional artifacts related to the current manuscripts and works of selected local artists enhance the exhibits.

Edward Waters College Museum, Obi Scott Umanna African Collection

Address: 1658 Old Kings Road
    Jacksonville, FL 32219
Hours: Monday–Friday 8–5
Admission: Free
Parking: Free
Phone: 904-470-8200

Edward Waters College, Florida's oldest independent, historically African-American institution of higher learning, was founded in Jacksonville in the 1870s. Like many other buildings in the city, it was destroyed in the great fire of 1901, only to be rebuilt on the present site on Old Kings Road. The imposing red-brick Centennial Building, completed in 1917, is the oldest building. It houses the college library and the small gallery that showcases the Obi Scott Umanna African Collection. This historical and anthropological collection consists of masks,

statues, musical instruments, and other items.

Florida Community College at Jacksonville, Kent Campus Art Gallery

Address: 3939 Roosevelt
    Boulevard
    Jacksonville, FL 32205
Hours: Monday–Thursday 10–4,
    Friday 10–3
Admission: Free
Parking: Free
Phone: 904-381-3674

Local and regional artists, many working in experimental media, computer-generated art, and new graphic techniques, present their works in the Kent Gallery. FCCJ's Kent Campus on the west side of the city is composed of a pleasingly integrated collection of brick buildings arranged around an enclosed plaza.

The Cummer Museum of Art and Gardens

Address: 829 Riverside Avenue
    Jacksonville, FL 32204
Features: Museum shop, gardens,
    library, concerts, lectures, coffee
    bar & bistro
Hours: Tuesday 10–9, Wednesday–
    Saturday 10–5, Sunday 12–5
Admission: Adults $10, seniors,
    students, and military $6, under
    age 5 free, Tuesday 4–9 free
Parking: Free, across from the
    museum
Phone: 904-356-6857
Website: www.cummer.org

The serene art museum overlooking the St. Johns

River includes collections of fine paintings, sculpture, and decorative art that encompass six thousand years. Galleries displaying works in the permanent collection are arranged by period, affording visitors a coherent view of the history of art. The large collection of rare Meissen porcelain is particularly outstanding. Programs and lectures are held in the auditorium, and several galleries are set aside for special exhibitions. One wing contains Art Connections, a lively interactive education center that makes learning about art a joyful experience. The museum is on the site of the former Cummer Mansion, and the original formal garden bordering the river is lovingly maintained.

Museum of Southern History

Address: 4304 Herschel Street
    Jacksonville, FL 32210
Features: Research library
Hours: Tuesday–Saturday 10–4
Admission: Adults $3, under age
    16 free
Parking: Free
Phone: 904-388-3574
Website: http://www.scv-kirby-
    smith.org/museum_history.htm

Dedicated to presenting the

lifestyle and culture of the antebellum South, this intimate museum was established by the Sons of Confederate Veterans in 1993. Artifacts, weapons, clothing, and memorabilia are displayed in thematic fashion, as are dioramas of Civil War battles, including the Battle of Olustee, the major engagement fought in Florida. A four-thousand-volume research library is located within the museum.

Lake City

Stroll through the restored downtown center of the county seat of Columbia County and admire the many handsome Victorian mansions in nearby historic neighborhoods.

Lake City-Columbia County Historical Museum

Address: 105 South Hernando
    Street
    Lake City, FL 32055
Hours: Wednesday 2–5 and Sat-
    urday 10–1
Admission: Free
Parking: Free
Phone: 386-755-9096

This two-story town house, built in the 1870s as a southern version of the rural-Italianate style, was saved from demolition to become a historical museum. For ninety-two years it was the home of May Vinzant Perkins, poet laureate of Florida. Graceful verandas at each level wrap around the house and seem to welcome visitors to stop and visit. Inside, period rooms display antique furnishings, clothing, and kitchenware. Other space is used to display historic weaponry and mementos of the Civil War and Reconstruction, as well as temporary thematic exhibits that focus on local heritage and history.

Lake City Community College, Levy Performing Arts Center

Address: 149 Southeast College
    Place
    Lake City, FL 32025
Parking: Free
Phone: 386-752-1822
Website: www.lakecitycc.edu

This modern facility on the spacious, pine-forested campus of Lake City Community College serves as the cultural center for the surrounding community. The seven-hundred-seat auditorium was completely renovated in 2007. In addition to performances by local groups, the Lyceum Series brings high-quality art, dance, music, and theater to the area. Children enjoy their own Theater for Young Audiences. Changing exhibits of the works of Florida artists are displayed on the curving walls of the Visual Arts Gallery on either side of the lobby.

Olustee

Olustee Battlefield Historic State Park

Physical Address: US 90, 15 miles
    east of Lake City
Mailing address: P.O. Box 40
    Olustee, FL 32072
Features: Nature trails
Hours: Daily 8–dusk; interpretive

center 9–5
Admission: Free
Parking: Free
Phone: 386-758-0400
Website: www.floridastateparks.
    org/olustee, www.battle
    ofolustee.org

The site of Florida's major Civil War battle is in the pine woods near Ocean Pond. Here, in 1864, approximately five thousand Confederates blocked the advance of 5,500 Federal troops intent on invading the state's interior and cutting off supplies of Florida beef and other food to the southern armies. A small interpretive center provides background information about the engagement through videos and displays of flags, uniforms, and artifacts. The battlefield is marked and a National Scenic Trail winds through the pines. The Battle of Olustee is reenacted each February, when hundreds of uniformed and costumed re-enactors set up camp for several days and relive the Civil War era. The camps are open to the public at times, and artillery experts demonstrate their authentic nineteenth-century cannons and field equipment.

Starke

Thanks to Santa Fe Community College, several key buildings in downtown Starke, including the imposing red-brick Bradford County Courthouse, have been restored for use as classrooms and offices. This community-minded effort has set the tone for the Call Street Historic District with its interesting shops and restaurants in the city's historic heart.

Eugene L. Matthews Bradford County Historical Museum

Address: 201 East Call Street
   Starke, FL 32091
Hours: Call for hours
Admission: Free
Parking: Free
Phone: 904-964-5382

Smile! One of the winsome displays in this museum features the studio of the Hoover Brothers, photographers in Starke for many years. Like the scenic views and portraits they left behind, other intriguing artifacts have been incorporated into displays that tell the story of this north Florida community. Named for Gene Matthews, editor of the *Bradford County Telegraph*, this museum presents well-designed exhibits that reveal the impact on Bradford County of the lumber industry, state prisons, and the massive influx of servicemen in training at nearby Camp Blanding during World War II. The museum is on the second floor of the historic Jones-Rosenberg Building, which has a pleasant walled garden with a gazebo on the east side.

Camp Blanding Museum and Memorial Park

Address: Route 1, Box 465,
   Camp Blanding
   Starke, FL 32091
Features: Picnic area, outdoor dis-
   plays and memorials
Hours: Tuesday–Sunday 12–4
Admission: Free

Parking: Free
Phone: 904-533-3196
Website: http://campblanding
   museum.org

During World War II, thousands of enlisted men were trained for infantry duty at Camp Blanding, most of them living in wood-based tents as they prepared for overseas service. Their life on the base, as well as the theaters of combat in Europe and Asia, are depicted in colorful exhibits and personal memorabilia in this military museum. The museum and adjacent park commemorate not only those infantrymen who served in World War II but also those who participated in subsequent conflicts. Veterans have donated much of the material on display in the museum, a refurbished barracks located next to Camp Blanding's main entrance. Within adjacent Memorial Park, a vintage airplane and army vehicles of many types are on display, and pathways lead to monuments honoring the infantry units that trained at Camp Blanding.

St. Augustine

As the nation's oldest city, St. Augustine proudly celebrates its place in history. Its rich colonial heritage is revealed in its carefully restored buildings, frequent festivals and historic reenactments, and sophisticated interpretive programs. This is where four hundred years of Florida history begins: give yourself plenty of time to absorb it. The Visitor Information Center across from the Castillo, the old fort, is a good place to start, with plenty of free maps and brochures and a film to orient visitors to the historic city.

Castillo de San Marcos National Monument

Address: 1 Castillo Drive South
St. Augustine, FL 32084
Features: Museum shop, ranger programs
Hours: Daily 8:45–5:15
Admission: Adults $7, under age 16 free
Parking: Parking lot with metered spaces
Phone: 904-829-6506
Website: www.nps.gov/casa

This massive fort built of coquina (a shell rock quarried nearby) has guarded St. Augustine for over three centuries. The Spanish built the fort; the British tried unsuccessfully to capture it, finally possessing it only when they acquired Florida in 1763; and the United States later used it to imprison Apache and Plains peoples. Within the rooms with high, rounded ceilings are displays related to various themes and historic periods, as well as to the daily lives of the men stationed here and to the role of coastal fortifications. Costumed National Park Service personnel and

volunteers interpret the history of the fortress and occasionally fire off the cannons and muskets. The views of the harbor and the city from the bastions have delighted tourists for many years. International visitors will find materials for self-guided tours in a variety of languages.

Ripley's Believe-It-Or-Not

Address: 19 San Marcos Avenue
St. Augustine, FL 32084
Features: Museum shop
Hours: Sunday–Thursday 9–7, Friday and Saturday 9–8
Admission: Adults $14.99, children $7.99
Parking: Free
Phone: 904-824-1606
Website: www.staugustine-ripleys. com

This popular tourist attraction is housed in the splendid Castle Warden, built in the 1880s for William Warden, a former partner of John D. Rockefeller and Henry Flagler. In 1950, the showplace mansion became the permanent home of Robert Ripley's unusual collection of curiosities, entertaining visitors with such unique items as, Egyptian mummies, shrunken heads, and other oddities. A recent addition is a Carrara marble replica of Michelangelo's sculpture, David.

Colonial Spanish Quarter Museum

Address: 29 St. George Street
St. Augustine, FL 32084
Features: Museum shop
Hours: Daily 9–5
Admission: Adults $6.89, seniors

$5.83, students aged 6–17
$4.24
Parking: Parking lots with metered
spaces
Phone: 904-825-6830
Website: historicstaugustine.com

Guides in period clothing recreate daily life in the 1740s in Old St. Augustine. Visit with the blacksmith, the carpenter or a soldier's wife as they go about their routine activities in this colonial period living history museum.

Casa Avero–St. Photios National Greek Orthodox Shrine

Address: 41 St. George Street
St. Augustine, FL 32084
Features: Museum shop, audiovisual presentation
Hours: Monday–Saturday 9–5,
Sunday 12–6
Admission: Free
Parking: Parking lot with metered
spaces
Phone: 904-829-8205,
800-222-5727
Website: www.stphotios.com

The story of Greeks in America is told in this museum, which is situated in a house associated with the earliest colony of Greek people established in this country in 1768.

Dr. Andrew Turnbull, a Scottish physician, recruited settlers from the Greek isles and other parts of the Mediterranean to work on his land in New Smyrna on Florida's Atlantic coast. Seeking a better life, they found instead such bad conditions that they eventually walked north to St. Augustine, where they settled permanently. The story of the courageous survivors, the Minorcans, is told here. The exquisite St. Photios Chapel, filled with Byzantine-style frescos, is rich in symbolic meaning. The Shrine, dedicated in 1982, is a tribute to traditional Greek culture and to the vitality of the Greek Orthodox Church in America.

Peña-Peck House

Address: 143 St. George Street
St. Augustine, FL 32084
Features: Museum shop, guided
tours
Hours: Monday–Saturday 10:30–
5:00; house tours 12:30–4
Admission: Free
Phone: 904-829-5064
Website: staugustinewomans-
exchange.com/house.shtml

This historic house located north of the Catholic Cathedral of St. Augustine was built as the residence of the Spanish Royal Treasurer, Juan Esteban de Peña, in the 1740s. Later owners changed and altered the house to suit their needs. What visitors see today is the restored town house, furnished in the 1830s' style and illustrating the life and times of the Peck family from Connecticut. Dr.

Seth Peck enlarged and improved the house and had his medical office on the first floor. The Woman's Exchange, a volunteer organization, maintains and operates the house.

Government House Museum

Address: 48 King Street,
St. Augustine, FL 32084
Hours: Monday-Sunday 9-3:45
Admission: Adults $2, students and children aged 6-12 $1
Phone: 904-825-5079

A colorful exhibit titled "The Dream, The Challenge, The City" introduces visitors to material that will make exploring the streets and environs of St. Augustine more meaningful. Maps, photographs, artifacts, and brief text cover five centuries of history, from early native settlements to the twentieth century.

Spanish Military Hospital Museum

Address: 3 Avilés Street
St. Augustine, FL 32084
Hours: Monday–Saturday 10–5, Sunday 12–5
Admission: Adults $3.50, seniors $3, children aged 6–18 $2
Phone: 904-827-0807
Website: www.spanishmilitary hospital.com

The atmosphere of a colonial military hospital is recreated in this small living-history museum: the office of the apothecary who prepared the medicines and grew his own medicinal herbs, the administrative office where patient records were kept, and

the ward where sick and injured patients were treated. This reconstructed building is on the site of the Hospital of Our Lady of Guadalupe, built during the Second Spanish Period.

Seguí-Kirby Smith House-St. Augustine Historical Society Research Library

Address: 6 Artillery Lane
St. Augustine, FL 32084
Hours: Tuesday–Friday 9–4:30
Admission: Free
Phone: 904-825-2333

A Minorcan merchant named Bernardo Seguí was the proud owner of this fine house of coquina stone and wood during the Second Spanish Period, and later it was the home of an American family. The city's first free public library was established here in 1895, and it is fitting that now the renovated and restored building serves as the repository of the excellent research collection of the Historical Society, founded in 1883.

Lightner Museum

Address: 75 King Street
St. Augustine, FL 32084
Features: Museum shop, café
Hours: Daily 9–5
Admission: $10, students and children age 12–18 $5, under age 12 free
Parking: Metered parking
Phone: 904-824-2874
Website: www.lightnermuseum.org
E-mail: info@lightnermuseum.org

The former Alcazar Hotel, built by railroad magnate Henry M.

Flagler, is now the sumptuous setting in which many priceless and eclectic collections are exhibited: everything from rare crystals and minerals to buttons and cigar bands. Included are outstanding examples of brilliant cut glass, antique furnishings, period costumes, mechanical musical machines (played daily at 11 and at 2), and lavish stained-glass works by Louis Comfort Tiffany. The Ballroom Gallery would make Cinderella swoon, and the Transition Gallery provides a glimpse of changing exhibits from the vast collections of Otto Lightner of Chicago, who believed everyone should collect something. Charming Victorian shop windows display a variety of artifacts of daily life from yesteryear. The building also houses a café and shops, installed in the former casino and swimming pool area. International visitors will be pleased to find interpretive materials in several languages.

Flagler College, Hotel Ponce de Leon

Address: 74 King Street
     St. Augustine, FL 32084
Features: Daily guided tours
Hours: Daily 10–3; visitors are restricted to the courtyards and lobby area except on guided tours
Phone: 904-819-6400
Website: www.legacy.flagler.edu

The Hotel Ponce de Leon was built by Henry Flagler in the late 1800s as the first of a chain of grand tourist hotels to accommodate passengers arriving in Florida on his new railroad. Flagler College, a private, liberal arts institution located in the former hotel, has preserved and restored many of the remarkable features of the building and grounds. The lobby, open to visitors all year, is very elegant indeed, and the dining hall has beautiful murals and Tiffany stained-glass windows. Join a tour and see these beautiful rooms at your leisure.

Ximenez-Fatio House Museum

Address: 20 Aviles Street
     St. Augustine, FL 32084
Features: Guided tours
Hours: Tuesday–Saturday, 11–4
Admission: Adults $5, seniors $3, students aged 6–17 $4
Phone: 904-829-3575

Florida's First Hotel is located

a block south of the Plaza. It is one of the best preserved of the few colonial buildings left in the Old City, built of coquina rock in 1798. The focus of the museum's interpretive program is on the period between 1830 and 1860 when it was a busy inn. Each room is decorated to represent a different sort of guest: a sea captain, an army officer, a family, and so on.

Old St. Augustine Village Museum

Address: 246 St. George Street (Corner of Cordova and Bridge Streets) St. Augustine, FL 32084
Hours: Monday–Saturday 9–4:30, Sunday 11–4:30
Admission: Adults $8.95, seniors $7.95, children $6.95, under age 5 free.
Phone: 904-823-9722
Website: www.old-staug-village. com

Historic buildings from other parts of the city were moved to the site and connected with attractive gardens and courtyards to form a pleasant urban complex. This city block of St. Augustine history includes nine furnished houses built between 1790 and 1910. Visitors may wander through the intriguing maze on self-guided tours.

St. Augustine Art Association

Address: 22 Marine Street St. Augustine, FL 32084
Hours: Tuesday–Saturday 12–4, Sunday 2–5
Admission: Free
Phone: 904-824-2310

Website: www.staa.org
E-mail: start@bellsouth.net

Art shows with a variety of themes change regularly in this visual arts center three blocks south of the Plaza. Enjoy the works of seasoned professional artists from the region, as well as original art created by students. Most of the shows are juried. Workshops in a variety of media are held throughout the year.

61

Oldest House Museum (Gonzalez-Alvarez House)

Address: 14 St. Francis Street St. Augustine, FL 32084
Features: Museum shop, guided tours
Hours: Daily 9–5, last tour at 4:30
Admission: Adults $8, seniors $7, students $4, families $18 (also includes Manucy Museum of St. Augustine History and Museum of Florida's Army)
Parking: Free
Phone: 904-824-2872
Website: www.staugustinehistor icalsociety.org/oldhouse.html

This venerable structure, which served as a private home for

more than 250 years, is organized in such a way that visitors move through the history of St. Augustine room by room, from the earliest Spanish period to the late 1880s, when the city was billed as "the winter Newport." Skilled guides conduct tours of the house every thirty minutes, explaining how it evolved from a one-story coquina dwelling for the Gonzalez family to its present form. The plants and trees in the spacious walled garden are labeled, and interpretive materials are available in a variety of foreign languages. Also included on the grounds (and in the entry fee) are two museums owned and operated by the St. Augustine Historical Society and a small gallery with changing exhibits. This is one of the most popular sites in St. Augustine.

Manucy Museum of St. Augustine History

The complex and changing events that made up the history of St. Augustine are explained with displays of carefully chosen artifacts and documents. The museum is named for Albert Manucy, a St. Augustine native and one of its most respected historians.

Museum of Florida's Army (Tovar House)

The military has had an enormous impact on St. Augustine, a garrison town. In the restored Tovar House, one of the city's oldest, figures of soldiers who served from the sixteenth to the twentieth century are on parade. Many company

rosters are also displayed. Check to see if any of your ancestors served in Florida's armies.

St. Augustine Lighthouse and Museum

Address: 81 Lighthouse Avenue
St. Augustine, FL 32080
Features: Museum shop, nearby park with playground, picnic area
Hours: Monday–Friday 9–6
Admission: Adults $8, seniors $7, children aged 7–11 $6 (children must be 7 years old and 4 feet tall to climb the tower); reduced fees to see the museum only
Parking: Free
Phone: 904-829-0745
Website: www.staugustinelight house.com
E-mail: info@ staugustinelight house.com

Drive across the Bridge of Lions to reach this restored 1888 navigational aid and landmark, which is painted in a dramatic spiral pattern of black and white. Visit the keeper's quarters, a restored two-story brick house that now contains exhibits, a period

room, and a video theater, to learn the story of the lightkeepers and the lights they tended. Visitors may climb the 219 steps to the top of the lighthouse tower, still maintained by the U.S. Coast Guard, to enjoy the panoramic view of St. Augustine.

Fort Matanzas National Monument

Address: 8635 A1A South
    St. Augustine, FL 32080
Features: Visitor center, video, ferry, nature trails, beach access
Hours: Daily 9–5:30
Admission: Free
Parking: Free
Phone: 904-471-0116
Website: www.nps.gov/foma

This small coquina fortress was built in the 1740s by the Spanish to protect St. Augustine from invasion from the south. Stop at the Visitor Center to see the exhibits and view the short video, then walk down to the dock on the Matanzas River. A passenger ferry takes visitors across the river to Rattlesnake Island where the fort is located. Guided tours by a National Park Service ranger will

reveal the history of this colonial outpost and the rugged life of the Spanish soldiers once stationed here. International visitors will find materials in several languages to add to their appreciation of this historic site.

Palm Coast

Washington Oaks Gardens State Park

Address: 6400 North Oceanshore Boulevard
    Palm Coast, FL 32137
Features: Beach access, nature trails, picnic area, visitor center, formal gardens
Admission: $4 per vehicle (up to 8 passengers)
Parking: Free
Phone: 386-446-6780
Website: www.floridastateparks. org/washingtonoaks

More than four hundred acres of pristine Florida, extending from the Atlantic Ocean to the Matanzas River, have been preserved in this park. The picturesque, boulder-strewn beach was created by the action of ocean waves washing away sand to expose coquina rock, an important building material during Florida's colonial era. Overlooking the tidal marshes of the Matanzas River to the west is an ornamental garden featuring exotic plants, roses, camellias, and azaleas. It is on the site of Belle Vista Plantation, whose owner was related by marriage to George Washington's family, hence the name.

Palatka

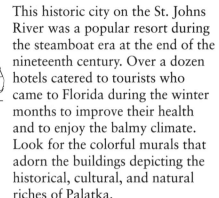

This historic city on the St. Johns River was a popular resort during the steamboat era at the end of the nineteenth century. Over a dozen hotels catered to tourists who came to Florida during the winter months to improve their health and to enjoy the balmy climate. Look for the colorful murals that adorn the buildings depicting the historical, cultural, and natural riches of Palatka.

Bronson-Mulholland House and Putnam County Historic Museum

Address: 100 Madison Street
    Palatka, FL 32178
Features: Guided tours
Hours: Tuesday, Thursday, and
    Sunday 2–5
Admission: Free
Parking: Free
Phone: 386-325-9825
Website: http://www.rootsweb.
    com/~flpchs/index.htm

Built before the Civil War by Judge Isaac Bronson, this Southern mansion has been restored and elegantly furnished with some original pieces. The house known as "Sunny Point" was designed to catch every fresh breeze, and the broad verandas afford a splendid

view of the St. Johns River. The attic dormers were used as a lookout post by Confederate soldiers, and later the house was occupied by Federal troops. After the Civil War, a friend of the Bronson family operated a school for children of freed slaves in the house. The adjacent historical museum is in the former officers' quarters of a fort used during the Seminole Wars. This 1830s building, moved from a nearby site, is used to interpret the rich history of Putnam County and the river that runs through it.

Larimer Arts Center

Address: 216 Reid Street
    Palatka, FL 32178
Hours: Monday–Thursday 10–4
Admission: Free
Parking: Free
Phone: 386-328-8998

This imposing building was a gift to the city of Palatka by Pittsburgh steel magnate James Mellon, who was a frequent visitor to the area. Built as a library in 1930, it features huge rounded windows and a small stage in the lobby. In 1993 it became the Larimer Arts Center, named for Mr. Mellon's wife, Rachel Larimer Mellon. Here the Arts Council of Greater Palatka offers classes, theatrical productions, dance programs, and changing gallery exhibits.

Ravine Gardens State Park

Address: 1600 Twigg Street
    Palatka, FL 32177
Features: Picnic area, hiking,
    bicycling

Hours: Daily 8–sundown
Admission: $4 per vehicle (up to 8 passengers)
Parking: Free
Phone: 386-329-3721
Website: www.floridastateparks. org/ravinegardens

Famous for the glorious azalea bloom in March and April, these gardens were created in 1933 as a federally funded project. More than sixteen hundred men labored to develop the park, to terrace its slopes, and to plant ornamental shrubs and trees in formal gardens and on meandering pathways leading around the ravine and along the spring-fed creeks. Near the entrance, a double colonnade built of native stone supports flowering vines, each pillar dedicated to one of the fifty states. A towering stone obelisk at the north end of this Court of States is dedicated to President Franklin D. Roosevelt, whose administration sponsored projects such as this to provide jobs and civic improvements. Drive around the ravine on the 1.8-mile-loop road or park and walk along the nature trails or across the bridges to enjoy the full impact of this botanical park. The Palatka Azalea Festival is held in early March at the peak of the azalea bloom, but the Ravine Gardens merit a visit at other times as well. Many native plants as well as blooming annuals can be admired here throughout the year.

St. Johns River Community College, Florida School of the Arts

Address: 5001 St. Johns Avenue
    Palatka, FL 32177
Hours: Gallery Monday–Friday
    8–5
Admission: Free
Parking: Free
Phone: 386-312-4300
Website: www.floarts.org

Theatrical, musical, and dance performances and exhibits of works by prominent Florida artists enrich the community that hosts Florida's first state-supported school of the arts. Established in 1974, FloArts provides talented high school and college students with special training appropriate to their artistic gifts. View the work of students and faculty, as well as regional artists, in the spacious Fine Arts Gallery, a vital component of the Florida School of the Arts.

Gainesville

As the home of Florida's flagship university and one of its largest community colleges, Gainesville is host to an outstanding number of cultural events. The community supports an exciting year-round calendar of music, drama, dance, and art events and festivals. Galleries, theaters, and a lively collection of outdoor cafés are centered in the downtown area, and nearby historic neighborhoods invite leisurely walking tours.

Santa Fe Community College, SFCC Art Gallery

Address: 3000 NW 83rd Street, Building M
Gainesville, FL 32606
Hours: Monday–Friday 12–4
Admission: Free
Parking: Free
Phone: 352-395-5464
Website: www.santafe.cc.fl.us

Invitational shows, thematic exhibitions, and selections of the best work of the award-winning art faculty fill the schedule of the SFCC Art Gallery, located at the heart of the spacious campus. Twelve exhibits throughout the year feature the work of faculty and students, and local artists. Lectures and colloquia are a part of the program of this visual arts resource that serves the community as well as SFCC students.

Hippodrome State Theatre

Address: 25 SE 2nd Place
Gainesville, FL 32601
Phone: Box office, 352-375-4477
Website: www.thehipp.org

Enjoy contemporary plays and the classics, starring gifted professional actors in this elegantly restored neoclassical building in the heart of downtown Gainesville. "The Hipp" is celebrating more than thirty-five years of presenting the best in live theatrical performances. With actors from across the nation and the Hippodrome's own roster of professional talent, eight mainstage shows are presented each year. An ongoing cinema series brings foreign and limited-release films to an appreciative audience. The Galleria in the lobby displays artwork by local artists.

The Thomas Center

Address: 306 NE 6th Avenue
Gainesville, FL 32601
Hours: Monday–Friday 9–5
Admission: Free
Parking: Free
Phone: 352-393-8539
Website: www.gvlculturalaffairs. org

Ask for a tour of this restored Mediterranean-revival cultural center in the heart of Gainesville's Northeast Historic District. You may encounter an exhibit of contemporary art, a jazz program, a modern dance recital, a chamber music concert, a nature lecture, or a wedding reception. The gardens surrounding the former luxury hotel have been handsomely restored; they invite the visitor to take a leisurely stroll or to simply stop and smell the roses.

Matheson Museum and Historic Matheson House

Address: 513 E. University Avenue
Gainesville, FL 32601
Features: Museum shop, research library
Hours: Tuesday–Friday 9:30–1:30, Sunday 1–5
Admission: Free
Parking: Free
Phone: 352-378-2280
Website: www.mathesonmuseum. org

The former American Legion Hall is now the museum and archives

of Alachua County history. The Matheson is in downtown Gainesville, adjacent to the Sweetwater Botanical Park and the historic Matheson House. The museum features an exhibition hall with both permanent and changing exhibits and a large library and archival research area. Interesting programs devoted to local history are open to the public. The 1850s Matheson House is open by appointment.

Morningside Nature Center

Address: 3540 E. University
   Avenue
   Gainesville, FL 32601
Features: Nature trails, picnic area,
   classes
Hours: Daily 9–5
Admission: No charge Monday–
   Friday; Saturday adults $2, chil-
   dren $1
Parking: Free
Phone: 352-334-2170
Website: www.cityofgainesville.org

Experience rural life of the late 1800s at this nature center and living-history farm. Say hello to the barnyard animals and visit the log cabin with its open hearth and sleeping loft, the turn-of-the-nineteenth-century kitchen, the blacksmith's shop, the old Half Moon schoolhouse, and the heirloom gardens. On weekends, costumed interpreters demonstrate traditional crafts and visitors can help feed the farm animals. Seasonal events include the Farm and Forest Festival each spring, the cane syrup boil in early December, and periodic sales of native plants. Put on your walking shoes, and explore seven miles of walking trails through a variety of north Florida ecosystems.

University of Florida, University Auditorium, Constans Theatre, and University Gallery

Physical Address: 400 SW 13th
   Street
   Gainesville, FL 32611
Hours: Gallery Tuesday–Friday
   10–5, Saturday 1–5
Admission: Free
Parking: Free; ask for a visitor's
   parking pass during the day
   Monday–Friday
Phone: Gallery 352-392-0201, UF
   box office 352-392-1653
Website: www.arts.ufl.edu/galleries

Art, drama, and music flourish on the campus of the state's largest university, part of which is listed as a historic district in the National Register of Historic Places. The Florida Players present contemporary and traditional productions year-round in the Constans Theatre next to the Reitz Union. The University Memorial Auditorium, an imposing Gothic-style structure, is the setting for classical music and jazz programs and guest lectures. Faculty and student art is exhibited in the University Gallery, alternating with traveling shows and shows assembled and curated at the gallery. Look for interesting shows of student work in the Reitz Union art gallery as well.

Samuel P. Harn Museum of Art

Address: Hull Road and SW 34th
    Street
    Gainesville, FL 32611
Mailing Address: P.O. Box 112700
Gainesville, FL 32611
Features: Museum shop, studio
    classes, lectures, guided tours,
    study center, Camillia Court
    Café
Hours: Tuesday–Friday 11–5, Sat-
    urday 10–5, Sunday 1–5
Admission: Free
Parking: $3 guest parking on
    weekdays, free on weekends
Phone: 352-392-9826
Website: www.harn.ufl.edu

Look for the huge statue of the Hammering Man in front of this splendid regional center for the visual arts located on the University of Florida Cultural Plaza. The Harn provides stunning exhibition space for shows that change at least a dozen times a year, thus creating a panorama of world art. The diverse collections assembled at the University of Florida over the past several decades—including works from the Americas, Asia, Africa, and Europe—serve as the nucleus of the ever-growing permanent collection. A multipurpose auditorium is designed for performances and educational programs, and an inviting educational area with a library and multimedia equipment encourages further exploration of the visual arts.

Florida Museum of Natural History, Powell Hall

Address: Hull Road and SW 34th
    Street
    Gainesville, FL 32611
Features: Museum shop, Butterfly
    Rain Forest
Hours: Monday–Saturday 10–5,
    Sunday and holidays 1–5
Admission: Donations—adults $6,
    seniors and students, $4, chil-
    dren aged 3–12 $2
Butterfly Rainforest: adults $8.50,
    seniors and students $6.50,
    children 3–12 $4.50
Parking: $3 guest parking on
    weekdays, free on weekends
Phone: 352-846-2000
Website: www.flmnh.ufl.edu

The official state museum of natural history has been located in Gainesville for almost a century. It is now located in Powell Hall, a visitor-friendly building on the Cultural Plaza located at the west edge of the University of Florida campus. The museum will introduce you to fascinating places, artifacts, and people: Florida's limestone caverns; ancient Florida fossils, the powerful Calusa people and their legacy of more than six thousand years of coastal fishing and the magical world of butterflies. Exceptional special exhibits bring the whole world into focus, whether it is the lives of bats or sharks, Tibetan tribal regalia, or Ice Age mammals. One of the world's major butterfly collections is housed here and live butterflies enchant visitors in a lush, tropical rainforest setting.

69

Phillips Center for the Performing Arts

Address: Hull Road and SW 34th
Street
Gainesville, FL 32611
Phone: 352-392-1900
Website: www.performingarts.ufl.edu

One of the most modern and well-equipped theaters in the Southeast is located on the Cultural Plaza adjacent to the Harn Museum and Powell Hall. A full schedule of opera, ballet, and classical music, as well as touring Broadway shows, popular artists, local companies, and programs for young audiences, keeps the community coming back for more. In addition to the main theater space, a black-box theater showcases experimental works.

Kanapaha Botanical Gardens

Address: 4700 SW 58th Drive
Gainesville, FL 32608
Features: Garden shop, picnic area, children's garden
Hours: Monday, Tuesday, Wednesday, and Friday 9–5, Saturday, and Sunday 9–dusk, closed Thursday
Admission: Adults $5, children aged 6–13 $3, under age 6 free
Parking: Free
Phone: 352-372-4981
Website: www.kanapaha.org

This superb botanical garden, one of the best in the Southeast, flourishes with colorful blooms year-round, inviting visitors to explore its water garden, cactus and palm gardens, heritage herb garden, fern-decked sunken garden, arbors of climbing vines, lakeside viewing sites, bamboo jungle, and seasonal surprises. Quaker naturalist William Bartram described the beautiful lake and surrounding area in his travel journal published in 1791; he would be equally impressed with the natural beauty of Kanapaha today. The newest feature is a children's garden.

Historic Haile Homestead

Address: 8500 Archer Road
Gainesville, FL 32608
Features: Guided tours
Hours: Saturday 10–2, Sunday
12–4
Admission: $5, under age 12 free
Phone: 352- 335-9096
Website: www.hailehomestead.org

The Haile Homestead was built in
1854 by Thomas and Serena Haile,
who moved to Alachua County
from Camden, South Carolina,
with their family and slaves to
establish a large cotton plantation.
They called their home Kanapaha,
but the Homestead is also known
as "The House with the Talking
Walls" because the Hailes and
their friends wrote on almost
every wall through the decades,
words that were preserved when
the antebellum house was restored
in the 1990s. Tours of the Haile
Homestead reveal not only insights
into the lives of the Hailes, but also
the enslaved people who built the
house and worked for the Haile
family after they were freed.

Newberry

Dudley Farm Historic State Park

Address: 18730 West Newberry
Road (State Road 26)
Newberry, FL 32669
Features: Visitor center, self-guided
tours, picnic area, nature trail
Hours: Wednesday–Sunday, 9–5
(farmstead closes at 4)
Admission: $4 per vehicle (up to 8
passengers)
Phone: 352-472-1142
Website: www.floridastateparks.
org/dudley

Dudley Farm is located west
of Gainesville. It was the home
of the Dudley family for three
generations, from the 1850s to the
1980s. The evocative and authentic
collection of nineteenth-century
wood frame buildings form the
centerpiece of the working farm,
a living history of rural life in
Florida. Fields are still plowed
with mules, crops are planted and
harvested, gardens are tended,
livestock is fed, quilts are stitched,
and each fall sugar cane is ground
and the cane juice cooked down to
sweet syrup.

Micanopy

Micanopy Historical Society Museum and Archives

Physical Address: Cholokka
Boulevard
Micanopy, FL 32667
Mailing Address: P.O. Box 462
Micanopy, FL 32667
Hours: Daily 1–4
Admission: Free
Parking: Free
Phone: 352-466-3200
Website: www.afn.org/~micanopy

The 1880s Thrasher Warehouse,
the home of this delightful
museum, is a treasure-house of
local history stretching back over
two hundred years. Micanopy,

named for a Seminole chief, is one of Florida's oldest towns: the site of a thriving Seminole village visited by naturalist William Bartram in the 1770s, and a frontier settlement during Florida's territorial period in the early 1800s. Artifacts from the Timucuan culture are arranged in intriguing displays, along with pioneer tools and household goods. A separate building on the grounds is the home of the Micanopy Archives. Take time for a walking tour of Micanopy, listed as a historic district in the National Register of Historic Places.

Archer

Archer Historical Society Railroad Museum

Address: Main Street and
   Magnolia Street
   Archer, FL 32618
Hours: Saturday 9–1
Admission: Free
Parking: Free
Phone: 352-495-1044
Website: www.yuleerailroaddays.
   org

The old yellow-and-green railroad depot, once the hub of commercial activity in Archer, is now a center dedicated to telling the story of the community's interesting people and past. Artifacts on display relate to the Civil War era, railroading, and the history of the African-American citizens of Archer. The annual Yulee Railroad Days Celebration in June honors David Levy Yulee, the railroad pioneer and first U.S. senator from Florida, who had a plantation in Archer in the 1860s.

Cross Creek

Named for the narrow creek linking Orange Lake and Lake Lockloosa, this refuge of simpler days and natural ways continues to draw those who are still looking for the Florida that used to be.

71

Marjorie Kinnan Rawlings Historic State Park

Address: 18700 County Road 325
   Cross Creek, FL 32640
Features: Guided house tours,
   nature trails, picnic area in ad-
   jacent county park
Hours: Grounds, daily 9–5; house
   tours Thursday–Sunday,
   hourly at 10, 11, 1, 2, 3, and 4,
   October–July
Admission: Guided house tours:
   adults $3, children aged 6–12
   $2, under age 6 free
Parking: $2 per vehicle
Phone: 352-466-3672
Website: www.floridastateparks.
   org/marjoriekinnanrawlings

The Cross Creek home of the Pulitzer Prize–winning author of *The Yearling* has retained its distinctive Florida Cracker style, right down to the chickens in the yard and the vegetables grown in the garden. The house is furnished

as it was when Marjorie Rawlings lived here: a typewriter like the one she used sits on the table on the front screened porch, and copies of the books she wrote here are on display in one of the rooms. Guides in 1930s period dress share stories of her life in Cross Creek and her literary world. The Marjorie Rawlings home is now a National Historic Landmark.

Hawthorne

The Gainesville to Hawthorne Trail is a fifteen-mile scenic corridor accessible to runners, hikers and bicyclists. The former railroad route, converted to a recreational trail, begins in Gainesville, crosses the north rim of Paynes Prairie, and leads to the quiet, uncongested town of Hawthorne, founded over a century ago.

Hawthorne Historical Museum and Cultural Center

Address: 7225 SE 221 Street
    Hawthorne, FL 32641
Hours: Wednesday and Friday, 10–2, Saturday and Sunday 1–4
Admission: Free
Parking: Free
Phone: 352-481-4491
Website: www.hawthorneflorida.org/museum

A historic church built in 1907 has been lovingly restored as a center for preserving and presenting Hawthorne's history. The original pulpit and pews are still in place, adding to the quiet charm and interest of the exhibits on display. The museum is two blocks from the trailhead of the Gainesville-Hawthorne Trail.

3. Central East Florida

Daytona Beach

Cocoa

Melbourne

Fort Pierce

Bunnell

Bulow Plantation Ruins

Address: P.O. Box 655
  Bunnell, FL 32110
Features: Picnic area, nature trails,
  canoe trail
Hours: Daily 9–5
Admission: $3 per vehicle Phone:
  386-517-2084
Website: www.floridastateparks.
  org/bulowplantation

Approach this dramatic historic site by way of a narrow road through a dense forest to discover the remains of a prosperous sugar plantation, which was established in the 1820s and then destroyed in 1836 during the Second Seminole War. The coquina ruins of the sugar mill indicate the impressive scale of this once-thriving plantation, which hosted John James Audubon on one of his collecting and painting trips through Florida. Signs explain the process of sugar production, and a small interpretive exhibit displays artifacts of the era. Explore the thirteen-mile loop of Bulow Creek by kayak or canoe.

Ormond Beach

Settled in 1902 by millionaires seeking a sunny vacation spot, Ormond Beach became a sporty resort when the wide beach was used by automobile enthusiasts to test early race cars.

The Casements

Address: 25 Riverside Drive
   Ormond Beach, FL 32176
Features: Museum shop, guided
   tours
Hours: Monday–Friday 9–5,
   Tuesday and Thursday 9–9,
   Saturday 9–noon
Admission: Free
Parking: Free
Phone: 386-676-3216
Website: www.thecasements.org
E-mail: thecasements@ormond
   beach.org

The former winter home of John D. Rockefeller has been restored and is now the cultural and civic center of Ormond Beach. The charming casement windows that give the house its name overlook a pleasant park and the Inland Waterway. A room has been restored with Rockefeller furnishings, and guides are happy to show visitors around the building. Ask to see the exhibits

of Boy Scout memorabilia and the Hungarian folk art on the upper floors. Art classes, exhibitions, lectures, and concerts are regularly scheduled.

Ormond Memorial Art Museum and Gardens

Address: 78 East Granada Boule-
   vard
   Ormond Beach, FL 32176
Features: Museum shop, classes,
   picnic area
Hours: Monday–Friday 10–4, Sat-
   urday and Sunday 12–4
Admission: $2 donation
Parking: Free parking to the rear
   of the gardens
Phone: 904-676-3347
Website: www.ormondartmuseum.
   org
E-mail: omam78@aol.com

This fine arts museum is set within a magnificent four-acre tropical garden with winding pathways, secret pools, and fountains. Several galleries in the museum display works of contemporary Florida artists in a variety of media. The OMAM opened in 1946 and honors those who served in both World Wars.

Daytona Beach

Billed as the "world's most famous beach," Daytona first gained fame early in this century when auto racers attained record-breaking speeds on its hard-packed sand. The tradition continues today on the Daytona International Speedway, where sleek racing cars still break records. Daytona Beach is divided by the Halifax River. For a treat on the ocean side, attend an outdoor concert at the ornate 1930s coquina bandshell, a restored oceanfront landmark. West of the Halifax River, enjoy a drive through Daytona's historic residential neighborhoods, shop in the restored downtown area, or stroll through the riverfront park.

Halifax Historical Museum

Address: 252 South Beach Street
 Daytona Beach, FL 32114
Features: Museum shop, research
 library
Hours: Tuesday–Saturday 10–4
Admission: Adults $4, children $1
Parking: Free parking in rear of
 building
Phone: 386-255-6976
Website: www.halifaxhistorical.org
E-mail: mail@halifaxhistorical.org

The classical entrance of the former Merchants Bank in historic downtown Daytona Beach, where the wealthy winter residents of Daytona once did their banking, now opens to a diverse collection of artifacts, dioramas, and memorabilia related to the history of Volusia County. The archives contain thousands of historic photos and postcards. Many fine interior features of the building have been preserved, including Tiffany-style stained-glass windows and skylights and original wall murals. Browse among the displays or view some of the extensive collection of historic videos.

Art League of Daytona Beach

Address: 433 South Palmetto
 Avenue
 Daytona Beach, FL 32114
Features: Classes, workshops
Hours: Gallery Tuesday–Sunday
 1–4 (winter)
Admission: Free
Parking: Free
Phone: 386-258-3856
Website: www.artleague.org

Founded in 1932, the Art League is one of the oldest art organizations in the state. The gallery, located in a contemporary building in Daytona Beach's historic district, exhibits the works of guest artists as well as of the talented student artists who study with outstanding instructors throughout the year. Workshops, demonstrations, and lectures complement the regular classes at this center for the visual arts.

Daytona Beach College, Southeast Museum of Photography

Address: 1200 West International
 Speedway Boulevard
 Daytona Beach, FL 32114
Hours: Tuesday, Thursday, Friday
 11–5, Wednesday 11–7,
 Saturday and Sunday 1–5;
 June, July, and December:
 Tuesday–Sunday 1–5
Admission: Free
Parking: Free
Phone: 386-506-4475
Website: www. smponline.org

Explore photography in all of its exciting and surprising aspects in this modern museum on the campus of Daytona Beach

College. The permanent collection contains the works of well-known artists such as Diane Arbus and Sally Mann, as well as historic examples of early and more recent photographic processes, from daguerreotypes to digital. Changing exhibits offer thought-provoking views of fine art photography and photojournalism by the country's top professionals. A reference archive and library provide opportunities for photographic research, while lectures, workshops, and children's programs promote public appreciation for photography.

Museum of Arts and Sciences

Address: 352 South Nova Road
  Daytona Beach, FL 32114
Features: Museum shop, nature
  trail, planetarium
Hours: Monday–Saturday 9–5,
  Sunday 11–5
Admission: Adults $12.95, seniors,
  children and students $6.95;
  free admission the first Tuesday
  of every month
Parking: Free
Phone: 386-255-0285
Website: www.moas.org

The Museum of Arts and Sciences has something to interest every visitor. Located in the ninety-acre Tuscawilla Nature Preserve, the museum houses a variety of exhibits ranging from the prehistoric to the contemporary. The American Wing showcases eighteenth- to twentieth-century decorative and fine arts by some of the nation's best artists and craftsmen, while the Cuban

Collection has paintings, crafts, and objects reflecting the cultural heritage of the people of Cuba. The skeleton of a 130,000-year-old giant sloth, unearthed not far from the museum, represents Florida's prehistoric era. There is a large collection of Americana on view, including two private railroad cars, and an interactive children's center.

Dunlawton Sugar Mill Botanical Gardens

Address: 950 Old Sugar Mill Road
  Daytona Beach, FL 32119
Features: Picnic area, botanical
  library
Hours: Daily 8–6
Admission: Free
Parking: Free
Phone: 386-767-1735
Website: www.dunlawton
  sugarmillgardens.org

This twelve-acre botanical garden combines native and exotic plants in a variety of settings with the remains of an early nineteenth-century sugar mill, destroyed during Seminole raids in 1836. Dunlawton Plantation was one of a series of coastal sugar-producing operations important to the state's economy during the territorial

period. Sugar cane is grown in the garden, and some of the machinery and equipment used in the processing of sugar are displayed.

Barberville

About halfway between Ocala and Daytona Beach on State Road 40, you might zip through this small community at the intersection of US 17. But stop and plan to spend a few hours here if you are seeking the "other Florida" that most tourists never find.

Pioneer Settlement for the Creative Arts

Address: 1776 Lightfoot Lane, Barberville, FL 32105
Features: Museum shop, picnic area, guided tours
Hours: Monday–Friday 9–4, Saturday 9–2
Admission: Adults $5, children $3
Parking: Free
Phone: 386-749-2959
Website: www.pioneersettlement. org

Step back into the past in this engaging village complex set

among the pine trees of rural Florida. The volunteer staff demonstrates weaving and spinning, blacksmithing, butter churning, soap making, and other pioneer arts. Wander around the Old Central School and enjoy the displays of toys, folk art, old tools, and artifacts of everyday living, or visit the country store to buy a souvenir. Also on the grounds are an old depot and a caboose, barns, a church, a turpentine still, and a bridge house, all of local historical significance.

DeLand

New York manufacturer Henry DeLand founded this city in 1878. Today it is best known for the university named for hatmaker John B. Stetson, who was also one of its great benefactors. Oak-shaded streets, handsome historic homes, and a downtown that has retained much of its historical integrity add to the attractions of this city.

Stetson University, Duncan Gallery of Art

Address: 123 East Minnesota Avenue
DeLand, FL 32723
Hours: Monday–Friday 10–4, Sunday 1–4 (closed in summer)
Admission: Free
Parking: Free
Phone: 386-822-7266

Exhibitions in a large gallery housed in historic Sampson Hall on the Stetson University campus include the works of nationally-known artists, student works, and a variety of pieces from the university's permanent collection.

Museum of Florida Art

Address: 600 North Woodland
   Boulevard
   DeLand, FL 32720
Features: Museum shop, tours,
   classes
Hours: Tuesday–Saturday 10–4,
   Sunday 1–4
Admission: $3, free on Sunday
Parking: Free
Phone: 386-734-4371
Website: www.delandmuseum.com
E-mail: info@delandmuseum.com

The Museum of Florida Art is located in DeLand's Cultural Arts Center across from the Stetson University campus. Changing exhibits in the five galleries showcase the works of Florida artists.

Gillespie Museum

Address: 234 Michigan Avenue
   DeLand, FL 32720
Features: Museum shop
Hours: September–May Tuesday–
   Friday 10–4, July–August by
   appointment only
Admission: Adults $2, children $1
Parking: Free
Phone: 386-822-7330

Website: www.gillespiemuseum.
   stetson.edu

The glow of giant quartz crystals; the mysteries of fossils embedded in stone; the brilliant colors of precious and semiprecious minerals such as malachite, lapis lazuli, and jasper; and splendid displays of unusual and exotic mineral specimens can be viewed in this museum, located in a historic house on the eastern edge of the Stetson University campus. Mr. and Mrs. Thomas B. Gillespie presented their outstanding collection—one of the largest and finest private collections of minerals in the world—to the university in the 1950s. Enjoy the new "Underground World"—a hard-rock mine exhibit.

Henry A. DeLand House Museum

Address: 137 West Michigan
   Avenue
   DeLand, FL 32720
Features: Research library
Hours: Tuesday–Saturday 12–4
Admission: Donation
Parking: Free
Phone: 386-740-6813
Website: www.delandhouse.com

Although the town of DeLand's founder never lived in this two-story, white-frame house, its role as a living museum introduces visitors to the town's history through artifacts and photographs. The house was for many years the home of Dr. Charles Farriss, a professor of Greek at Stetson University who had a flair for working with leaded and stained

glass. The excellent results can be seen in many parts of the house, which is tastefully furnished with period pieces donated by area residents. A reference library has been established in an adjacent building by the West Volusia Historical Society.

African American Museum of the Arts

Address: 325 South Clara Avenue
DeLand, FL 32721
Hours: Wednesday–Saturday 10–4
Admission: Free
Parking: Free
Phone: 904-736-4004
Website: www.africanmuseum deland.org
E-mail: info@ africanmuseum deland.org

A small collection of African art, along with space for changing exhibits featuring the works of established and emerging artists, represents a resource that reaches out to bring visual arts to the community. The museum's unique role in the area is due to its primary focus: the arts and culture of African and Caribbean Americans.

Ponce Inlet

Ponce de Leon Inlet Lighthouse and Museum

Address: 4931 South Peninsula
    Drive
    Ponce Inlet, FL 32127
Features: Museum shop, nature
    trail
Hours: Daily 10–6
Admission: Adults $5, under age
    11 $1.50
Parking: Free
Phone: 386-761-1821
Website: www.ponceinlet.org

Explore one of Florida's most complete light stations, which has guarded the inlet to the Halifax River for over a century. The centerpiece of this restored complex is the 175-foot red-brick lighthouse itself, whose light flashed for the first time in 1887. Climb 203 steps to the top for a breathtaking view. Visitors may take guided or self-guided tours of the buildings on the site to learn about the coastal sentinels' importance to the state's economy.

New Smyrna Beach

An indigo plantation was established here by a company of English investors during Florida's brief British period (1763–1784), with colonists imported from the Mediterranean. When the enterprise failed, most of the workers fled to St. Augustine, where they found refuge.

Atlantic Center for the Arts

Address: 1414 Art Center Avenue
New Smyrna Beach, FL 32168
Hours: Monday–Friday 10–4,
Saturday 10–2
Admission: Free
Parking: Free
Phone: 386-427-6975
Website: www.atlanticcenterfor
thearts.org

This interdisciplinary artists' community sits on sixty-seven acres of lush tropical vegetation bordering a pristine bay. Dedicated to promoting artistic excellence, the center provides research and development opportunities for renowned master artists-in-residence and for the talented associates selected to work with them. On the grounds are artists' residences, a variety of studios, a theater, and a library. The lofty art gallery provides public exhibition space for the works of exceptional artists.

Titusville

North Brevard Historical Museum

Address: 301 South Washington
Street
Titusville, FL 32796
Hours: Tuesday–Saturday 10–3
Admission: Free
Parking: Free
Phone: 312-269-3658
Website: www.nbbd.
com/godo/history

A former store in the historic downtown section of Titusville has been converted into a museum of local history. Long before the days of the space program, Titusville was a thriving winter tourist center on the Indian River. Photographs and postcards, clothing and household artifacts, tools, and technological curiosities reveal glimpses of the past.

Valiant Air Command Warbird Aviation Museum

Address: 6600 Tico Road
Titusville, FL 32780
Features: Museum shop
Hours: Daily 9–5
Admission: Adults $12, seniors
and military $10, children $5
Parking: Free
Phone: 321-268-1941

Join the Valiant Air Command in celebrating the preservation of America's aviation heritage. In this museum dedicated to the people who flew and maintained military aircraft, historic displays related to the wars of the twentieth century bring back memories. In addition to the dozen or so aircraft in the display and restoration hangars and out on the parking area, many of them in flying condition, there are exhibits of aircraft engines, vintage flying gear, uniforms, and aviation memorabilia. Interpretive materials are available in a number of languages.

Kennedy Space Center Visitor Complex

Address: Kennedy Space Center,
FL 32899
Features: Museum shops, cafés,
free kennels, strollers, and
wheelchairs
Hours: Opens daily at 9 a.m., but
closing times vary according to

the season
Admission: Adults $38 plus tax, children aged 3–11 $28 plus tax; fee includes the Astronaut Hall of Fame
Parking: Free
Phone: 321-449-4444
Website: www.kennedyspace center.com

People come from all over the world to relive the drama of space exploration and see the actual sites where astronauts lift off for their journeys into space. Strap in for a day of space exploration at Kennedy Space Center Visitor Complex. Go vertical on the new Shuttle Launch Experience to discover the sights, sounds, and sensations of launching into space. Be prepared for an inspiring experience with tours venturing deep into NASA's spaceport facilities, daily Astronaut Encounters, towering rockets, and IMAX® space films. Admission includes the U.S. Astronaut Hall of Fame® featuring astronaut memorabilia, simulators, and displays.

Cocoa

With shady arcades and patios and a variety of shops and restaurants, Cocoa Village invites visitors to linger in its historic downtown area. Drive along the scenic River Road, Florida's finest waterfront avenue, and admire views of the Indian River that captivated winter-weary northern visitors a century ago.

Library of Florida History

Address: 435 Brevard Avenue Cocoa, FL 32922
Hours: Tuesday–Saturday 10–4
Admission: Free
Parking: Free
Phone: 321-690-1971
Website: www.florida-historical-society.org

The Florida Historical Society has established its extensive library collection in the old Federal Building in Cocoa Village. Books, maps, photographs, and a wide range of valuable documents are available for scholarly, genealogical, or personal research. Changing exhibits related to the history of Florida are displayed.

Brevard Museum of History and Natural Science

Address: 2201 Michigan Avenue Cocoa, FL 32926
Features: Museum shop, nature trail, picnic area
Hours: Monday–Saturday 10–4, Sunday 12–4
Admission: Adults $6, seniors and military $5.50, children aged 3–16 $4.50

Parking: Free
Phone: 321-632-1830
Website: www.brevardmuseum.
  com

The progress of regional settlement and the natural history of Brevard County are interwoven in this comprehensive museum. Permanent displays of the tools and artifacts of early humans (including the work of archaeologists who uncovered the seven-thousand-year-old Windover site), of Seminole culture, and of pioneer life along the Indian River complement exhibits of sea life, shells, and local flora and fauna. Special traveling exhibitions are featured, and the Discovery Room invites children to learn with hands-on activities. The twenty-two-acre Nature Preserve south of the building has pathways leading through three Florida ecosystems: a pine sandhill, an oak hammock, and a freshwater swamp.

Melbourne

Named for the Australian city (the birthplace of the town's first postmaster), this technology center spreads westward from the shores of the Indian River. Historic neighborhoods along the riverfront have an "Old Florida" ambiance, but this city definitely has its eye on the future as well.

Maxwell C. King Center for the Performing Arts

Address: 3865 North Wickham
  Road
  Melbourne, FL 32935
Phone: 321-242-2219
Website: www.kingcenter.com

This stylish, modern performance space with two thousand seats brings big Broadway shows, concerts, dance, and assorted entertainment options to the Treasure Coast. There is also a small black box theater. Dramatic walls of glass and a canopied entryway define the architectural direction of this distinctive performing arts center. Amenities include an art gallery in the lobby and a hospitable mezzanine for between-acts congregating.

Brevard Art Museum

Address: 1463 Highland Avenue
  Melbourne, FL 32935
Features: Museum shop, classes,
  lectures, guided tours
Hours: Tuesday-Saturday 10–5,
  Sunday 1–5
Admission: Adults $5, seniors $3,
  students $2, free on Thursday
  1–5
Parking: Free
Phone: 321-242-0737
Website: www.brevardartmuseum.
  org

The modern museum building overlooks Pineapple Park and the Indian River in the Eau Gallie historic district. Seven spacious galleries offer well-lighted space for works from the growing permanent and distinguished visiting collections. Knowledgeable docents are on hand to interpret the exhibitions, and they are one of the strongest assets of this ever-expanding visual arts center. Lectures and programs are held in the adjacent Harris Auditorium.

Vero Beach

Located in a county famed for its citrus production and the quality of its fruit, this city also enjoys high marks for its quality of life. Polo, sport fishing, yachting, and golf are favorite activities. This would have amazed the pioneers who first settled along the Indian River, who were dependent on their own resources and hard work to survive.

McLarty Treasure Museum

Address: 13180 North A1A
     Vero Beach, FL 32963
Features: Observation deck over-
     looking the ocean
Hours: Daily 10–4:30
Admission: $1, under age 6 free
Parking: Free
Phone: 772-589-2147
Website: www.floridastateparks.
     org/sebastianinlet

In 1715, a fierce hurricane struck a fleet of Spanish treasure ships sailing back to Europe laden with gold and silver from the New World. Some fifteen hundred survivors of the shipwreck struggled to shore on this sliver of Florida coast, and the precious cargo sank to the floor of the ocean. This museum, which overlooks the watery site of the disaster, chronicles the fate of the survivors and the saga of how the treasure was retrieved over the years. Using modern equipment, treasure divers are still recovering valuable eighteenth-century items and artifacts from the sea, many of which are on display. The McLarty is a feature of the Sebastian Inlet State Park.

Indian River Citrus Museum

Address: 2140 14th Avenue
     Vero Beach, FL 32960
Features: Museum shop, play-
     ground, picnic area
Hours: Tuesday–Friday 10–4
Admission: Free
Parking: Free
Phone: 772-770-2263
Website: http://veroheritage.org/
     CitrusMuseum.html
E-mail: info@ veroheritage.org

Indian River Citrus! Bags of bright, juicy, sweet oranges and tangy grapefruit offered at fruit stands have tempted travelers to load up the trunks of their cars for generations. The Spanish introduced oranges to Florida during the colonial period, and today citrus is a $200 million industry. This small museum tells the story of citrus pioneers, special citrus varieties, local groves, pickers, packing houses, and citrus crate labels. It is located in a pleasant park next to the Heritage Center, the hub of community activities since the 1920s.

Vero Beach Museum of Art

Address: 3001 Riverside Park
   Drive
   Vero Beach, FL 32963
Features: Museum shop, classes,
   programs, research library,
   guided tours Wednesday–
   Sunday 1:30–3:30
Hours: Monday–Saturday10–4:30,
   Sunday 1–4:30
Admission: $2 donation
Parking: Free
Phone: 772-231-0707
Website: www.vbmuseum.com

The largest cultural arts facility
of its kind on Florida's Treasure
Coast offers national and
international art exhibitions
throughout the year. Three
galleries, as well as sculpture
gardens and open areas, offer
opportunities to enjoy art alfresco.
The permanent collection is
devoted to the works of American
artists, and a challenging
exhibition schedule brings a
variety of new works—as well as
cultural celebrations related to the
shows—to the whole community.
Concerts, films, live performances,
and lectures are offered in the
auditorium, and studio classes
taught by professional art
instructors are also scheduled.

Fort Pierce

Named for a fort built during the
Seminole War era, this city on
the Indian River called itself the
"Pineapple Capital of the World"
at the turn of the last century.

Harbor Branch Oceanographic Institution

Address: 5600 US 1 North
   Fort Pierce, FL 34946
Features: Museum shop, guided
   tours, picnic area
Hours: Monday-Friday 10–5
Admission: Adults $10, children
   aged 4–13 $6 under age 3 free
Parking: Free
Phone772-465-2400
Website: www.hboi.edu

North of Fort Pierce is an
extensive complex devoted to
oceanographic research. Through
museum exhibits and tours of
the facilities, the public is invited
to come aboard to learn more
about the oceans of the world
and how they affect our lives.
In this unusual science center,
visitors of all ages can explore
the underwater frontiers in
aquaculture, biomedical research,
ocean exploration, and many other
phases of marine science.

St. Lucie County Historical Museum

Address: 414 Seaway Drive
   Fort Pierce, FL 34950
Features: Museum shop, reference
   library, guided tours
Hours: Tuesday–Saturday 10–4,
   Sunday 12–4
Admission: Adults $4, seniors
   $3.50, children $1.50
Parking: Free
Phone: 772-462-1795
Website: www.st-lucie.lib.
   fl.us/museum

The museum opens a window
to the past, offering glimpses of
the history of the early Treasure
Coast area. The lives of the pre-
Columbian Ais people, Seminole
Indians, ranchers, fishermen,
farmers, and townspeople are
revealed in artful permanent
exhibits, including a new one
on World War II activities in
Fort Pierce. The many hands-on
experiences invite visitors to touch
the past, and the Special Exhibition
Gallery features a variety of
changing exhibits. Enjoy a guided
tour the restored Gardner home,
built in 1907, for engaging insights
into turn-of-the-nineteenth-century
lifestyles along the Indian River.

A. E. "Bean" Backus Museum and Gallery

Address: 500 North Indian River
   Drive
   Fort Pierce, FL 34948
Features: Museum shop
Hours: Tuesday–Saturday 10–4,
   Sunday 12–4
Admission: Free
Parking: Free
Phone: 772-465-0630
Website: www.backusmuseum.com
E-mail: info@backusmuseum.com

This museum and gallery is
dedicated to Florida landscape
artist A. E. "Bean" Backus. Many
of his works, which are part of the
museum's permanent collection,
are shown in one of the museum's
galleries. Three other galleries
show changing exhibits of the
works of contemporary artists.

Manatee Observation and Education Center

Address: 480 North Indian River
   Drive
   Fort Pierce, FL 34948
Features: Museum shop, observa-
   tion tower, wildlife boat tour,
   picnic area
Hours: Tuesday–Saturday 10–5,
   Sunday 12–4 (January–June),
   Thursday–Saturday 10–5
   (July–September), Tuesday–
   Saturday 10–5, Sun 12–4
   (October–December)
Admission: $1
Parking: Free
Phone: 772-466-1600
Website: www.manateecenter.com

Located on Moore's Creek and the
Indian River, the Manatee Center

offers a waterfront observation area where manatees may be seen in their natural habitat. This environmental education center seeks to preserve not only the manatees but also the fragile ecosystem on which they depend.

UDT-SEAL Museum

Address: 3300 North AIA
    Fort Pierce, FL 34949
Features: Museum store
Hours: Tuesday–Saturday 10–4,
    Sunday 12–4, Monday 10–4
    (January–April)
Admission: Adults $6, children
    aged 6–12 $3
Parking: Free
Phone: 772-595-5845
Website: www.navysealmuseum.
    com

The earliest training of the Naval Combat Demolition Units began in the 1940s in Fort Pierce, and this unique museum vividly tells the story of Navy frogmen, members of the Underwater Demolition Teams (UDTs), and Navy SEALs

(an acronym for sea, air, and land). Underwater vessels and other special watercraft used in naval warfare from World War II to Desert Storm, as well as a Navy helicopter, are part of the two-acre outdoor display. Inside, a collection of diving gear, weapons, demolition gear, and memorabilia is displayed. The arduous training of the SEALs, which prepares them for unconventional warfare that may involve reconnaissance or underwater demolition, is shown in photographs and action-filled videos.

4. Central Florida

Ocala

Orlando

Lakeland

Sebring

Ocala

Even before the Civil War, tourists journeyed by boat down the Ocklawaha River to view Silver Springs, one of Florida's most famous natural attractions, just east of Ocala. Canoeing is popular on the Silver River, and Ocala National Forest draws many who enjoy hiking and camping. Surrounded by rolling horse-farm countryside, Ocala is growing rapidly in population and is also expanding its cultural resources.

Appleton Museum of Art

Address: 4333 East Silver Springs
    Boulevard
    Ocala, FL 34470
Features: Museum shop, lectures, concerts, film series, art reference library, guided tours
Hours: Tuesday–Saturday 10–5,
    Sunday 12–5
Admission: Adults $6, seniors and
    students $4, under age 11 $3
Parking: Free
Phone: 352-291-4455
Website: www.appletonmuseum.org

A work of art in itself, this classic glass-and-marble building is a cultural cornerstone for Ocala. The museum was a gift from art collector and retired industrialist Arthur Appleton. The Appleton Museum houses over six thousand works of art from his collection, reflecting more than five thousand years of art history. The permanent collection features eighteenth-

and nineteenth-century art from Europe and North America; pre-Columbian, African, and Asian artwork; antiquities; and international contemporary art. Changing exhibitions are presented quarterly, and the museum auditorium is the venue for the film series and lectures.

Silver River Museum and Environmental Education Center

Address: 1445 Northeast 58th
   Avenue
   Ocala, FL 34470
Features: Museum store, picnic
   area, nature trails, reference
   library
Hours: Saturday and Sunday 9–5
   all year; Tuesday–Friday in
   June and July
Admission: Museum: $2 per
   person, under age 6 free
Parking: State park entry fee $4
   per vehicle
Phone: 352-236-5401
Website: www.SilverRiver
   Museum.com

The Silver River winds along the edge of this five-thousand-acre nature preserve, a Florida State Park that celebrates Florida's pioneer heritage as well as its ecological treasures. A Cracker settlement—composed of a simply furnished cabin, barns, outbuildings, and a school that doubles as a church—introduces visitors to how early homesteaders survived by their own ingenuity and hard work. The nearby Silver River Museum is used during the week for school programs but is open to the public on the weekends, as is the extensive reference library. Exhibits in the museum focus on local prehistory, history, and ecology, while miles of nature trails wind through sand pine scrub, hardwood hammocks, wetlands, and swamps, finally ending down at the Silver River. Birdwatchers and photographers will find this an especially rewarding place to spend a day.

Don Garlits Museum of Drag Racing

Address: 13700 Southwest 16th
   Avenue
   Ocala, FL 34473
Hours: Daily 9-5, closed Christmas
Admission: Adults $15, seniors
   and students $13, aged 5–12
   $6, under 5 free
Parking: Free
Phone: 352-245-8661
Website: www.garlits.com

"Big Daddy" Don Garlits, the king of U.S. drag racing, has assembled a vast collection of fast cars, stock cars, drag racers, and funny cars, as well as antique automobiles. Car buffs will be enthralled by the rooms full of engines, mementos of races and racing gear, trophies, displays of original tools and equipment, models and prototypes, and a replica of Don's garage, where many innovations in modern auto racing began.

There are two large buildings, one dedicated to antique cars, the other to auto racing.

Bushnell

Dade Battlefield Historic State Park

Address: 7200 South Battlefield
   Drive (County Road 603)
   Bushnell, FL 33513
Features: Picnic area, nature trails
Hours: Park daily 8–sundown;
   museum daily 9–5
Admission: $2 per vehicle, $1 on
   foot or bicycle
Parking: Free
Phone: 352-793-4781
Website: www.floridastateparks.
   org/dadebattlefield

The peaceful, oak-shaded park commemorates a violent encounter—one that led to the Second Seminole War—between Seminoles and the U.S. Army on December 28, 1835. On the military trail between Tampa and Ocala, 107 soldiers commanded by Major Francis Dade were ambushed by Seminole warriors resisting planned removal of the tribe to Oklahoma. The battle is reenacted annually in late December with vivid realism. During the battle weekend, both sides, suitably clad in either uniforms or Seminole attire, set

up camp and welcome the public with displays of armament and weapons, military drills, and war dances. An interpretive museum tells the story of the skirmish, while permanent markers and a replica of the log breastwork erected by the soldiers indicate the battle site.

Leesburg

The city is named for the Lee family that settled here more than 130 years ago. Rolling hills and large lakes connected by creeks and canals, many of them with interesting historical associations, are appealing natural attractions in this central-ridge section of Florida.

Lake-Sumter Community College, Art Gallery and Paul P. Williams Fine Arts Theatre

Address: 9501 US Highway 441
   Leesburg, FL 34788
Hours: Gallery Monday–Friday
   10–5
Parking: Free
Phone: 352-356-3506

The atmosphere is friendly on this seventy-acre campus on Silver Lake. Performances by theater students bring drama and cultural enrichment to county schools and the community. In addition, a series encompassing Broadway specials, professional concerts, ballet, opera, and theater programs is performed in the 417-seat Fine Arts Theatre. The Art Gallery exhibits the works of contemporary Florida artists.

Tavares

The county seat of Lake County, located in Florida's geographic center, derives its name from a Portuguese word meaning "hub." It is on a narrow strip of land between Lake Dora and Lake Eustis, where boating and fishing are the major pastimes. An interesting excursion, particularly worthwhile for bird lovers, is a boat trip through the Dora Canal and the chain of heritage lakes that gives this county its name.

Lake County Historical Museum

Address: 317 West Main Street
  Tavares, FL 32778
Features: Resource library and
  archives
Hours: Monday–Friday 8:30–5
Admission: Free
Parking: Free
Phone: 352-343-9600

The main floor of the restored Lake County Courthouse, built in 1924, is now a regional museum. Exhibits highlight the history of the towns and cities of Lake County. Tools and implements made by the earliest known settlers, the native Timucuans, are on display, while pioneer artifacts, dioramas, and photographs depict the importance of ranching and citrus production to the area's development.

Eustis

Eustis Historical Museum

Address: 536 North Bay Street
  Eustis, FL 32726
Hours: Monday–Friday 1–5, first

Saturday of every month 12–4
Admission: Donation
Parking: Free
Phone: 352-483-0046
Website: www.eustishistorical
  museum.com

A meander through the imposing fourteen-room Clifford House, built in 1910-1911 on the shore of Lake Eustis, adds to the pleasure of a visit to this historic museum. Sit a spell on one of the rockers on the broad, open front porch and savor the feeling of the less hectic life enjoyed by Floridians early in the century. Elegant furnishings, lace curtains, and fine woodwork distinguish the interior, and topical exhibits reveal interesting insights into this central Florida community. In the former carriage house, the Citrus Museum displays items and exhibits related to the era before hard winter freezes when Eustis was the citrus capital of the world.

Mount Dora

Wealthy northerners discovered this hilly site overlooking Lake Dora in the 1880s, and it still retains the character of an exclusive resort village. The Antique Boat Festival in March is an outstanding event that attracts well over 150 vintage watercraft owners, many attired in the sporty fashions of past eras, who delight in showing off their lovingly restored and preserved wooden boats. This "town that time forgot" has a busy schedule of other festivals devoted to bicycles, antiques, and art.

Mount Dora Center for the Arts

Address: 138 East 5th Avenue
    Mount Dora, FL 32757
Hours: Monday–Friday 10–4, Saturday 10–2
Admission: Free
Parking: Free
Phone: 352-383-0880
Website: www.mountdora
    centerforthearts.org

This community art center offers exhibition space for central Florida artists and provides workshops and educational programs related to the visual arts for people of all ages. Located in the heart of the historic downtown, the Center for the Arts has as its main event the Mount Dora Arts Festival, held each February since 1975. The festival now draws more than 250,000 visitors from around the state to enjoy Mount Dora's cultural and historic attractions.

Sanford

Founded by developer Henry Sanford late in the nineteenth century as an agricultural and citrus center, this city on the southern shore of Lake Monroe was the site of Fort Mellon during the Second Seminole War. Enjoy a walking tour of downtown Sanford, with its turn-of-the-nineteenth-century architecture and pleasant mix of cafés, art galleries, and antique shops.

Sanford Museum

Address: 520 East 1st Street
    Sanford, FL 32771
Hours: Tuesday–Friday 11–4, Saturday 1–4
Admission: Free
Parking: Free
Phone: 407-302-1000
Website: http://www.ci.sanford.
    fl.us/cf03.html

This restored Mediterranean-revival-style stucco building houses period furnishings, paintings, and historic memorabilia. It also contains a manuscript collection of more than fifty-five thousand items related to the career of Henry S. Sanford (1823–1891), the distinguished lawyer and diplomat for whom the city is named. The museum is located in Fort Mellon Park on the Lake Monroe waterfront.

Seminole County Public Schools Student Museum

Address: 301 West 7th Street
    Sanford, FL 32771
Hours: Monday–Friday 1:30–4
Admission: Free

Parking: Free
Phone: 407-320-0520
Website: http://www.millennium.
scps.k12.fl.us/smuseum.html

This Center for the Social
Studies is in a handsome, brick,
Romanesque revival–style school
built in 1902 as the Sanford
High School. It is the fourth-
oldest school in continuous use
in the state, offering Seminole
County children a unique learning
opportunity. Activities and tours
that engage children in active
learning are scheduled for the
morning hours, and various rooms
devoted to Native American and
pioneer life, an early twentieth-
century schoolroom, and
"Grandma's Attic" add depth and
dimension. The museum is open to
the public in the afternoon.

Museum of Seminole County History

Address: 300 Bush Boulevard
Sanford, FL 32773
Features: Research library
Hours: Monday–Friday 9–5, Sat-
urday 9–4
Admission: Free
Parking: Free
Phone: 407-665-2489
Website: www.seminolecountyfl.
gov/hs/museum

The museum complex is comprised
of two buildings. One is the former
County Home for the Poor, built
in 1926 and referred to locally as
"The Old Folks' Home." Extensive
collections of artifacts and
memorabilia are on display, and
historic photographs line the walls.
Enjoy a leisurely tour of the period

rooms and areas devoted to the
history of transportation and the
Second Seminole War. The second
building focuses on the agriculture
and industries of the area: citrus,
celery, ferns, turpentine, lumber,
cattle, and commercial fishing.

Seminole Community College, Fine Arts Theater, Concert Hall, and Fine Art Gallery

Address: 100 Weldon Boulevard
Sanford, FL 32773
Hours: Gallery Monday–Thursday
9–4
Admission: Gallery free
Parking: Free
Phone: 407-708-2704
Website: www.seminole.cc.fl.us

This cultural complex located
on the spacious SCC campus
offers exciting programs in the
performing and visual arts,
which merit the attention of the
fast-growing local and student
populations. The Fine Arts
Theater, which seats two hundred,
presents challenging theatrical
productions, some followed by
"Talk Backs" with the director,
cast, and crew. Choral and
symphonic concerts performed by
students and guest artists, many of
them free of charge, are held in the
360-seat Fine Arts Concert Hall.
The SCC Fine Art Gallery exhibits
the works of major Florida artists
and those of students and faculty.
The gallery is open during the day
and on evenings when concerts are
scheduled.

Maitland

The Maitland Art Center

Address: 231 West Packwood
Avenue
Maitland, FL 32751
Features: Museum shop, classes
Hours: Monday–Friday 9–4:30,
Saturday and Sunday 12–4:30
Admission Adults $2, seniors and
students $2
Parking: Free
Phone: 407-539-2181
Website: www.maitlandartcenter.
org

Described as one of America's
best examples of "fantastic
architecture," this beautifully
preserved art center, recognized
today as both a state and national
historic site, celebrates a long
tradition of nurturing avant-garde
art. The Aztec-inspired art deco
decorations created by André
Smith and his associates have
been carefully preserved in the
unique Artists' Village. Smith, an
architect and award-winning artist,
designed and built the village in
the 1930s as the Research Studio,
where young resident guest artists
could develop their talents and
display their works. He would
be proud today of the stature
and variety of art exhibited, as
works of contemporary regional,

national, and international artists
are shown to fine effect in the
intimate galleries Smith designed.
Classes and workshops fill the
small studios in a year-round
program open to all ages, and an
annual children's art festival is
held on the grounds each spring,
another tradition André Smith
would probably applaud. The
serene open-air Garden Chapel
and Mayan Courtyard, with its
evocative original sculpture and
lush tropical landscaping, is a
favorite spot for weddings and
private parties.

93

Maitland Historical Society Museum and Telephone Museum

Address: 221 West Packwood
Avenue
Maitland, FL 32751
Hours: Thursday and Friday 12–4,
Saturday and Sunday 10–4
Admission: Adults $3 children $ 2
Parking: Free
Phone: 407-644-2541

The museum, which is located
in a small white cottage, houses
an eclectic collection of artifacts,
textiles, and photographs relating
the history of Maitland. The
Telephone Museum contains an
interesting collection of telephones
and communication equipment,
some dating back to 1910, when
the Maitland Telephone Exchange
was established by an enterprising
grocer who encouraged his
customers to install telephones in
their homes so they could call in
their grocery orders.

Waterhouse Residence and Carpentry Shop Museums

Address: 820 Lake Lily Drive
    Maitland, FL 32751
Hours: Thursday and Friday 12–4,
    Saturday and Sunday 10–4
Admission: Adults $3, children $2
Parking: Free
Phone: 407-644-2451

William Waterhouse, a Union Army veteran from New York, brought his family to the village of Maitland in the 1880s. A skilled carpenter and builder, he constructed many of the early homes in Maitland, including his own residence on the shore of Lake Lily. Now a house museum, it warmly reflects the way of life enjoyed by this middle-class family during Florida's late Victorian period. You can almost hear the voices of the children at their chores or at play and the rustle of Mrs. Waterhouse's starched skirts on the stairs as you visit this charming home. Equally fascinating, especially to those intrigued with turn-of-the-nineteenth-century tools and technology, is Mr. Waterhouse's carpentry shop behind the house. The small building has been restored and stocked with a marvelous selection of woodworking tools. Tour guides

demonstrate the use of select hand tools, some of them owned by Mr. Waterhouse himself.

Eatonville

Zora Neale Hurston National Museum of Fine Art

Address: 227 East
    Kennedy Boulevard
    Eatonville, FL 32751
Hours: Monday–Friday 9–4
Admission: Free
Parking: Free
Phone: 407-647-3307
Website: www.zorafestival.com/
    museumhome.html

This art museum is located in Eatonville, the hometown of charismatic African-American writer, folklorist, and anthropologist Zora Neale Hurston. It serves as the entry point to the art, culture, and history of Eatonville, the oldest incorporated African-American municipality in the United States. The creative works of established and promising artists of African descent are showcased in changing exhibits on a year-round basis. Each January, a festival to honor Zora Neale Hurston is held in Eatonville: it is a celebration of her contributions as well as those of other African-Americans.

Winter Park

One hundred years ago, New Englanders seeking a healthy climate and investment opportunities settled in this lake-studded area, establishing schools, churches, a college, a library, and other cultural amenities. Today, this city just north of Orlando contains some of Florida's loveliest neighborhoods and shopping districts. The annual Spring Sidewalk Art Festival in March is one of the country's best, with top-juried artists and craftsmen competing for handsome prizes.

Morse Museum of American Art

Address: 445 Park Avenue
  Winter Park, FL 32789
Features: Museum shop, guided tours
Hours: Tuesday–Saturday 9:30–4, Sunday 1–4, Friday 4–8 November–April
Admission: Adults $3, students $1, under age 12 free
Parking: Free
Phone: 407-645-5311

Be prepared for a stunning experience as you step into this museum, glowing with the artistic glassworks of Louis Comfort Tiffany. The Morse Tiffany collection, said to be the most comprehensive in the world, includes leaded-glass windows, blown glass, lamps, pottery, paintings, jewelry, and enamel work. The museum also houses an important collection of American art pottery and representative collections of nineteenth- and twentieth-century American paintings and decorative art. The 1932 Tiffany Chapel, created in 1893, is one of the American master's most impressive installations.

95

Cornell Fine Arts Museum

Address: 1000 Holt Avenue,
  Rollins College
  Winter Park, FL 32789
Features: Guided tours, lectures
Hours: Tuesday–Saturday 10–5, Sunday 1–5
Admission: Adults $5
Parking: Free
Phone: 407-646-2526
Website: www.rollins.edu/cfam

Located on the attractive campus of Rollins College on the shores of Lake Virginia, this facility has a distinguished permanent collection of more than six thousand works of art. A rich variety of media and artists are presented in changing exhibits. Lectures, guided tours, and a concerts-in-the-gallery series are scheduled to complement the shows.

Annie Russell Theatre

Address: Rollins College
  Winter Park, FL 32789
Phone: 407-646-2501
Website: www.rollins.edu/theatre

Dedicated to Annie Russell, a famous early twentieth-century actress, this elegant Mediterranean-style theater is one of the architectural landmarks on the Rollins College campus.

The Annie Russell hosts four productions per year by the Department of Theater and Dance, and a spring dance concert.

Albin Polasek Foundation Museum

Address: 633 Osceola Avenue
   Winter Park, FL 32789
Hours: Wednesday–Saturday 10–4,
   Sunday 1–4, closed July and
   August
Admission: Adults $5, seniors $4,
   children $3
Parking: Free
Phone: 407-647-6294
Website: www.polasek.org

The legacy of Czech-American sculptor Albin Polasek is presented in more than two hundred works displayed in landscaped gardens, part of his estate on the shores of Lake Osceola. The complex also includes a studio, two galleries, and a chapel.

Crealdé School of Art

Address: 600 St.
   Andrews Boulevard
   Winter Park, FL 32792
Hours: Monday–Friday 9–5, Sat-
   urday 9–1
Admission: Free
Parking: Free
Phone: 407-671-1886
Website: www.crealde.org

The galleries at the Crealdé School of Art exhibit the works of established and emerging artists, and the outdoor sculpture garden provides a pleasing venue for the works of Florida sculptors. Classes and workshops for all ages in a variety of media—from painting and photography to drawing and three-dimensional art—are offered throughout the year. The Crealdé also partners with the city of Winter Park in operating the Hannibal Square Heritage Center, which features the art and culture of the city's African-American community.

Christmas

Fort Christmas Historical Park

Address: 1300 Fort Christmas
   Road (SR 420)
   Christmas, FL 32709
Features: Museum shop, research
   library, picnic area, playground
Hours: Museum Tuesday–Saturday
   10–5, Sunday 1–5
Admission: Free
Parking: Free
Phone: 407-568-4149

Capture the historical texture of a rugged military outpost at this replica of the fort. The original fort was built in late December 1837, during the Second Seminole War, as a supply depot and rebuilt in the mid-1970s as a Bicentennial project. The stockade and blockhouses constructed of massive logs encompass the parade grounds as well as the store building, which now houses a research library. One blockhouse exhibit area focuses on the Seminole War period; the other is devoted to honoring the pioneer heritage of the community. Also on the park grounds are a Cracker cabin, a rustic ranch house, farm implements, and a sugar cane grinder, all reminders of the 1880s settlement era. Picnic shelters, a playground, and a ball field make this all-purpose park perfect for a family outing.

Orlando

Once a quiet, conservative, citrus-growing center, Orlando has become a world-class tourist magnet with an international reputation. More and more attractions and theme parks are built each year, offering the visitor a bewildering variety of choices. In addition, there is an array of cultural, historical, and natural attractions in the "real Orlando." Look for art in the Orlando City Hall and at many other public sites throughout the city; historic neighborhoods clustered around tranquil lakes; fine museums, parks, and gardens; vital college campuses; and vigorous theaters and concert halls. Many local attractions provide interpretive materials and tour guides in a variety of languages for the growing number of foreign visitors drawn to this dazzling vacation destination.

Harry P. Leu Gardens and Leu House

Address: 1720 North Forest
   Avenue
   Orlando, FL 32803

Features: Garden shop, guided
   tours of Leu House
Hours: Garden daily 9–5; house
   tours 10–3:30; closed July
Admission: Adults $5, children $1;
   free Monday 9–12
Parking: Free
Phone: 407-246-2620
Website: www.leugardens.org

97

This fifty-six-acre botanical park features a vast array of plants in natural settings, including the largest documented collection of camellias in the southeastern United States; display greenhouses; a xerophyte garden; a floral clock; Florida native plants; and miles of scenic walkways, shaded by massive oak trees. The new Garden House on the shores of Lake Rowena graciously welcomes visitors and provides space for classes and lectures, a venue for special events, a botanical library, and a brightly blooming Garden Shop. In the heart of the gardens is the restored Leu House Museum, expanded from an 1880s pioneer farmhouse to an elegant mansion, now open to the public for guided tours.

The house and gardens were a gift to the city from Orlando businessman Harry P. Leu, an avid collector of exotic plants, who developed the gardens over a twenty-five-year period. In many ways, the story of the owners of this fascinating house and property mirrors the growth of Orlando from a small center for citrus and agriculture to a sophisticated metropolis. The lakeside docks are favorite spots for bird watchers and the formal rose garden (the largest in Florida), first planted by Mary Jane Leu, attracts many admirers who come to experience the beauty and fragrance of the numerous varieties of Mrs. Leu's favorite flower.

Orlando Science Center

Address: 777 East Princeton Street
  Orlando, FL 32803
Features: Museum shop, café
Hours: Sunday–Thursday 10–6,
  Friday and Saturday 10–9
Admission: Adults $14.95, children aged 3-11 $9.95 (additional fees for films, planetarium show)
Parking: Adjacent parking structure $4
Phone: 407-514-2000 (toll-free 888-672-4386)
Website: www.osc.org
E-mail: info@osc.org

The Orlando Science Center invites you to have fun with science with hundreds of interactive, hands-on exhibits that explore our universe, near and far. Here you can travel through the human body or take a tour of our solar system and beyond. The elegant OSC opened in 1997 and has won raves (and repeat visits) from area families. Live theater, big screen movies, and laser shows in the CineDome, a bustling KidsTown for the youngest set, a Florida swamp complete with its own live critters, and one of Florida's largest observatories are some of the center's attractions. A knowledgeable cadre of docents and the "Young Einsteins," recruited from local schools, are on hand to make sure visitors get the most out of their discovery adventures at the Orlando Science Center.

Orlando Repertory Theatre

Address: 1001 East Princeton Street
  Orlando, FL 32803
Parking: Free
Phone: 407-896-7365
Website: www.orlandorep.com

Central Florida's oldest and largest theater complex, conveniently located in beautiful Loch Haven Park, has something for everyone excited by live theatrical performance. The Mainstage Series offers critically acclaimed productions of the best of Broadway; the REP Youth Academy provides theatre education for children; and the UCF Conservatory presents UCF'S MFA students in productions for young audiences.

Mennello Museum of American Art

Address: 900 East Princeton Street
  Orlando, FL 32803
Hours: Tuesday–Saturday 10:30–4:30, Sunday 12–4:30
Admission: Adults $4, seniors $3, students $1, under age 12 free
Parking: Free
Phone 407-246-4278
Website: www.mennellomuseum.org

The gorgeous lakeside setting of the Mennello is embellished with fanciful, whimsical sculpture. Colorful paintings by Earl Cunningham form the core of the permanent collection, but other traditional, folk, and contemporary artists are celebrated in this young-at-heart museum, which opened in Loch Haven Park in 1998.

Orlando Museum of Art

Address: 2416 North Mills Avenue
    Orlando, FL 32803
Features: Museum shop
Hours: Tuesday–Saturday 10–4,
    Sunday 12–4
Admission: Adults $8, seniors $7,
    children aged 6–18 $5
Parking: Free
Phone: 407-896-4231
Website: www.omart.org
E-mail: info@omart.org

Important collections of nineteenth- and twentieth-century American art, art of the ancient Americas, and African art are on permanent display at the museum. Outstanding curated and touring exhibitions are hosted in the large galleries of this major regional art museum, which also presents a year-round series of educational programs for the community.

Orange County Regional History Center

Address: 65 East Central Blvd
    Orlando, FL 32801
Features: Museum shop
Hours: Monday–Saturday, 10–5,
    Sunday 12–5
Admission: Adults $7, seniors and
    students $6.00, children aged
    3–12 $3.50
Parking: Free 2 hours parking in
    adjacent Public Library garage
    with paid admission

Phone: 407-836-8500,
    800-965-2030
Website: www.thehistorycenter.org

Step back in time and discover the past that led to today's tourist-centric community. The History Center, dedicated to keeping the spirit of local history alive, is located in the 1929 Orange County Courthouse in downtown Orlando. Visitors embark on a journey through Orlando's transition from Indian Settlement to a small town surrounded by groves and cattle ranches to a twenty-first-century mecca for tourists from all over the world. Nationally important, limited-run exhibitions are also presented at the Center.

University of Central Florida, Art Gallery

Address: 4000 Central Florida
    Boulevard
    Orlando, FL 32817
Hours: Monday–Friday 9–4
Admission: Free
Parking: $5 fee, purchase permits
    in parking lots or Parking Ser-
    vices Center
Phone: 407-823-3161
Website: www.art.ucf.edu

The Visual Arts Building on the UCF campus presents art created by student, faculty, and visiting artists in its main gallery, and displays works in progress on the walls of the second-story atrium. Exhibits change often and present interesting views of emerging art trends and of traditional and experimental approaches to the visual arts. The UCF campus, its buildings arranged in a circular pattern with parking on the outer edge, was designed to preserve several unique Florida ecosystems.

Kissimmee

Cattle ranching has long been an important part of life in Kissimmee. The Silver Spurs Rodeo recalls the colorful days when Florida cow hunters rounded up their free-roaming herds for branding each spring. Florida beef supplied the Confederate Army, and tough little scrub cows, descendants of cattle introduced by the Spanish, were shipped by the thousands to Cuba in the 1800s.

Pioneer Center Museum

Address: 750 North Bass Road
    Kissimmee, FL 34746
Features: Museum store, picnic
    area, nature trails
Hours: Thursday–Saturday 10–4,
    Sunday 1–4
Admission: Adults $2, children
    aged 6–12 $1
Parking: Free
Phone: 407-396-8644

Relax on the porch of the spacious Cracker cabin built in 1899 and envision the long-gone pioneer days of Kissimmee, before it became a gateway to modern attractions. Surrounded by an orange grove, the complex of buildings includes a museum and a one-room country store. It also serves as headquarters for the Osceola County Historical Society, which maintains a library and a research center on the oak-shaded grounds.

Osceola Center for the Arts

Address: 2411 East Irlo Bronson
    Memorial Highway
    Kissimmee, FL 34744
Hours: Monday–Friday 9–5, Sat-
    urday 9–12
Admission: Free
Parking: Free
Phone: 407-846-6257
Website: www.ocfta.com

This contemporary cultural center located between Kissimmee and St. Cloud serves as the official arts and cultural center for Osceola County and encompasses a theater and an art gallery. The 244-seat theater, the home of the Osceola Players, has been completely renovated, and the art galleries bracketing the theater feature changing exhibitions and works of regional artists.

Polk City

Fantasy of Flight

Address: 1400 Broadway
    Boulevard Southeast
    Polk City, FL 33868
Features: Museum store, restau-
    rant, aircraft and balloon rides,
    research archives
Hours: Daily 10–5

Admission: Adults $26.95, seniors
$24.95, children aged 6–15
$13.95, extra for flight time
Parking: Free
Phone: 863-984-3500
Website: www.fantasyofflight.com

A stunning art deco facility is
home to a collection of over forty
vintage aircraft, many restored
to flyable condition. Guided
tours include visits to working
restoration and maintenance areas.
Climb inside the cockpit of a
Corsair fighter for a battle over the
Pacific and take a spin in the hang-
glide simulator for a thrilling ride.

Lakeland

This city lives up to its name,
making the most of the beautiful
lakes within its boundaries.
Mayfaire-by-the-Lake is a spring
arts event on Lake Morton;
historic buildings and a restored
art deco promenade enhance Lake
Mirror; and a unique architectural
complex designed by Frank
Lloyd Wright overlooks Lake
Hollingsworth.

Polk Museum of Art

Address: 800 East Palmetto Street
Lakeland, FL 33801
Features: Museum shop, research
library
Hours: Tuesday–Saturday 10–5,
Sunday 1–5

Admission: Adults $5, seniors $4
Parking: Free
Phone: 863-688-7743
Website: www.PolkMuseumofArt.
org

Excitement starts at the front door:
the large entry hall is hung with
eye-catching works of art. The
museum's permanent collection
contains twentieth-century
American art, with an emphasis on
contemporary Florida artists, as
well as pre-Columbian and Asian
art. The sculpture garden is visible
through huge windows, and nine
galleries draw the visitor toward
the permanent exhibits and toward
others set aside for changing
shows. The modern facility has
well-equipped classrooms and
a large auditorium for films,
programs, and performances.

Florida Southern College, Frank Lloyd Wright Visitor Center, and Melvin Gallery

Address: 111 Lake Hollingsworth
Drive
Lakeland, FL 33801
Hours: FLW Visitor Center
Monday–Friday 10–4, Melvin
Gallery Monday–Friday 9–4
Admission: Free
Parking: Free
Phone: 863-680-4110
Website: www.flsouthern.edu

Students helped build some of
these striking contemporary
structures designed by American
architect Frank Lloyd Wright and
constructed over a twenty-year
period on the campus of this small

planes designed for air races, stunt planes, one-of-a-kind airplanes, and exhibits related to general aviation in Florida fill the large hangar. This is a popular place for "fly-ins," sociable gatherings of private pilots and aviation buffs who enjoy sharing their love of flying.

private college. The Frank Lloyd Wright Visitor Center displays the influential architect's work, and a self-guided walking tour introduces visitors to the unique educational complex Wright called "Child of the Sun." Major restoration has been completed, including the great dome-shaped fountain designed by Wright as a centerpiece. The 1,800-seat Branscomb Memorial Auditorium, the Buckner Theater, and the Melvin Gallery are performing and visual arts centers serving the college and the community.

Sun 'n' Fun Air Museum

Address: 4175 Medulla Road
   Lakeland, FL 33807
Hours: Monday–Friday 9–5, Sat-
   urday 10–4, Sunday 12–4
Admission: Adults $8, seniors $6,
   students aged 8–12 $4
Parking: Free
Phone: 863-644-0741
Website: www.sun-n-fun.org

The world of sport aviation is the main focus of this engaging museum located on the southwest edge of the Lakeland Airport. Colorful experimental aircraft,

Winter Haven

Polk Community College, Fine Arts Gallery and Theater

Address: 999 Avenue H, Northeast
   Winter Haven, FL 33881
Hours: Gallery Monday–Friday
   10–2
Admission: Free
Parking: Free
Phone: Gallery 863-297-1050; box
   office 863-297-1050

Visual and performing arts events are held in the Fine Arts Complex on the PCC campus located on the northwest shore of Lake Elbert. The Fine Arts Gallery exhibits shows that change monthly, while the five-hundred-seat auditorium is the ideal setting for Special Performances, the annual series featuring professional talent, and other theatrical and musical groups.

Lake Wales

Historic Bok Sanctuary

Address: 1151 Tower Boulevard
Lake Wales, FL 33853
Features: Museum and garden
shop, free wheelchairs and
strollers, café, nature trails,
picnic area
Hours: Daily 8–6 (no admission
after 5)
Admission: Adults $10, children
aged 5–12 $3, under age 5 free
Parking: Free
Phone: 863-676-1408
Website: www.boksanctuary.org
E-mail: info@boksanctuary.org

Bok Tower stands on the highest
point in peninsular Florida, a quiet
sanctuary and a unique monument
combining the beauty of music,
nature, and art. Dedicated in 1929
to the American people, the tower
and the surrounding 250-acre
gardens were the gift of publisher
and writer Edward W. Bok. The
carillon plays throughout the
day, with a carillon recital each
day at 1 and 3 P.M. The tranquil
gardens, which are home to many
species of wildlife, were designed
by the Olmsted Firm, the creators
of New York's Central Park.
The Singing Tower, its image
shimmering in the long reflecting
pool, was built of Georgia marble
and Florida coquina stone and
embellished with sculpture,
decorative grillwork, and massive
bronze doors depicting Creation.
The new visitor center features
an introductory film and exhibits
and models that explain how
the carillon works. Also on
the grounds are the Pinewood
House and Gardens, outstanding
examples of Mediterranean-revival
architecture and landscaping.

The Depot, Lake Wales Museum and Cultural Center

Address: 325 South Scenic
Highway
Lake Wales, FL 33853
Features: Museum shop
Hours: Monday–Friday 9–5, Sat-
urday 10–4
Admission: Free
Parking: Free
Phone: 863-678-4209
Website: www.cityoflakewales.
com/depot

Located along the CSX Historic Corridor in downtown Lake Wales, its vivid pink stucco walls and red Mediterranean tile roof draw attention to this 1920s Atlantic Coast Line Railroad passenger station, now a treasure-filled showcase of historic memorabilia. Permanent exhibits define the importance of citrus, cattle, and turpentine to the area's development, while photographs and authentic equipment and furnishings recreate railroad history. The railroad theme is heightened by the vintage railcars on display. Rotating exhibits feature vintage clothing, displays of Native American culture, patriotic memorabilia, and a fall quilt show. The art gallery features the creative works of local artists, adding further interest to this community cultural center.

Lake Wales Arts Center

Address: 1099 SR 60 East
    Lake Wales, FL 33853
Features: Museum shop, classes,
    concerts
Hours: Monday–Friday 9–4 all
    year; Saturday 10–4, Sunday 1–
    4 (September 1–May 31)
Admission: Free
Parking: Free
Phone: 863-676-8426
Website: www.lakewalesartscenter.
    org

The former Holy Spirit Catholic Church, a landmark mission-style building constructed in 1927, is now a Polk County center for art and music. Family programs, Sunday afternoon lectures, concerts, and a series of art exhibitions keep the Arts Center busy throughout the year. Workshops in a variety of media are offered, and an annual outdoor art show held in March on the shores of Lake Wales is an outstanding cultural community event.

Bartow

Homeland Heritage Park

Physical address: Corner of Church
    Street and 2nd Avenue
    Homeland, FL
Mailing address: Drawer CS07,
    Box 7005
    Bartow, FL 33831
Features: Picnic area
Hours: Monday–Friday 8–5
Admission: Free
Parking: Free
Phone: 863-534-3766

Beginning with the preservation of the old Homeland Academy, the Heritage Park, which is located near Bartow, expanded with the addition of a log cabin and barn dating back to 1888; a wood-frame homestead built at the same time by the affluent Blocker family; and the Bethel Methodist Church, restored to its late-1880s appearance, complete with the original stained-glass windows. The five-acre complex is in Homeland, an old farming community that grew up and prospered around the Bethel Church in the late nineteenth century.

Mulberry

Mulberry Phosphate Museum

Address: SR 37 and Southeast 1st
Street
Mulberry, FL 33860
Hours: Tuesday–Saturday 10–4:30
Admission: Donation
Parking: Free
Phone: 863-425-2823
Website: www.mulberrychamber.
org/attractions.htm

Mulberry is known as the
phosphate capital of the world.
In this museum, visitors find an
outstanding collection of fossilized
remains of flora and fauna
discovered in the process of mining
for phosphate, a valuable mineral
that underlies the surface of much
of this part of Florida. Educational
exhibits explain how phosphate is
mined, and the skeletons of a ten-
million-year-old whale and other
prehistoric sea creatures remind us
that the peninsula of Florida used
to lie beneath the ocean. As the
museum grows, more of the story
of this ancient "Bone Valley" will
be revealed.

Sebring

Scenic Lake Jackson is the focal
point of this town in the heart of
Florida's citrus belt. The Cultural
Center encompasses the library,
civic center, theater, and art gallery,
clustered around a spacious park
on the east shore of the lake. The
lavishly landscaped town circle a
few blocks away is the hub of the
historic commercial district.

Highlands Museum of the Arts

Address: 351 West Center Avenue
Sebring, FL 33870
Hours: Monday–Friday 9–4
Admission: Free
Parking: Free
Phone: 863-385-5312
Website: www.highlandsartleague.
com

A modern, two-story art museum
on the shores of Lake Jackson,
influenced by the Mediterranean
style of architecture that was so
popular in Florida in the 1920s,
is the center for visual arts in this
area.

Children's Museum of the Highlands

Address: 219 North Ridgewood
Drive
Sebring, FL 33870
Hours: Tuesday–Saturday 10–5,
Thursday 10–8
Admission: $3
Parking: Free
Phone: 863-385-5437
Website: www.childrensmuseum
highlands.com

This museum is a lively space for
children to explore their world
in a safe learning environment. A
miniature store, bank, post office,
and medical office are open for
business, and aspiring thespians
can play with puppets or try

on costumes and expand their dramatic skills in the little theater. The One World Diner is a winner with young visitors who pretend to prepare and serve foods from all over the world to their parents and peers.

Civilian Conservation Corps (CCC) Museum

Address: 5931 Hammock Road
    Highlands Hammock State
    Park
    Sebring, FL 33872
Hours: Museum daily 9:30–3:30
Admission: Park $4 per vehicle (up
    to 8 passengers)
Parking: Free
Phone: 863-386-6094
Website: www.floridastateparks.
    org/highlandshammock

One of the more successful federal programs created under the New Deal was the Civilian Conservation Corps (CCC), which provided more than three million young men with wages, skills, education, and meaningful work during the Great Depression. Between 1933 and 1942, the CCC helped develop eight hundred state parks, created miles of hiking trails, built hundreds of cabins and lodges, restored historic structures, and planted millions of trees. Located in a rustic building built by the CCC in Highlands Hammock State Park, this museum reflects the impact of the men who laid the groundwork for Florida's fine system of state parks in the 1930s.

5. Central West Florida

Crystal River
Dade City
Tampa
St. Petersburg
Bradenton
Sarasota

Inverness

Old Courthouse Heritage Museum

Address: 1 Courthouse Square
    Inverness, FL 34450
Features: Museum store, archives
Hours: Monday–Friday 10–4, Sat-
    urday 10–3
Admission: Free
Phone: 352-341-6429
Website: www.citrushistorical.org

The yellow brick Citrus County
courthouse with its distinctive
copper cupola, built in 1912,
stands in the heart of downtown
Inverness. Permanent exhibits
feature the prehistory of Florida
and the pioneering spirit of
those who settled Citrus County.
Changing exhibits are also on view.
Movie buffs will enjoy a visit to the
meticulously restored courtroom
on the second floor, where scenes
from the 1961 movie *Follow That
Dream*, starring Elvis Presley, were
filmed.

Crystal River

Fishing in the Gulf of Mexico
and diving into the clear, spring-
fed waters that attract the gentle
manatee entice visitors to this fast-
growing community. Archaeological
evidence indicates that prehistoric
humans discovered the natural
advantages of this coastal paradise
over two thousand years ago.

Crystal River Archaeological State Park

Address: 3400 North Museum Point
Crystal River, FL 34428
Features: Museum shop, picnic area
Hours: Daily 8–sundown, museum 9–5
Admission: $2 per vehicle
Parking: Free
Phone: 352-795-3817
Website: www.floridastateparks.org/crystalriver

This site was occupied by native Floridians for sixteen hundred years before Europeans landed on the peninsula. It was a ceremonial complex of temple and burial mounds and middens, which were created over the centuries as the Native Americans discarded oyster and other seafood shells. A possible solar observatory with stelae, or ceremonial stones, links these peoples to others in the Americas who worshiped the sun and studied the celestial tapestry to understand their gods. A small museum interprets the evidence uncovered here and places it in a global context. Visitors may climb the impressive temple mound and follow trails to other points of interest.

Coastal Heritage Museum

Address: 532 Citrus Avenue
Crystal River, FL 34429
Hours: Tuesday–Friday 11–3, Saturday 9–2
Admission: Donation
Parking: Free
Phone: 352-795-1755
Website: www.citrushistorical.org/museums.asp

The Citrus County Historical Society's coastal region museum is in the Old City Hall, a limestone rock building constructed as a Works Progress Administration (WPA) project in 1939. The building once held the offices of the mayor, fire chief, chief of police, and city clerk, and three jail cells. A detailed diorama of Crystal River in 1927, memorabilia, photographs, and artifacts tell the story of this Gulf coast community.

Homosassa

Homosassa Springs Wildlife State Park

Address: 4150 South Suncoast Boulevard
Homosassa, FL 34446
Features: Museum shop, café, picnic area, educational center, nature trails
Hours: Daily 9–5:30
Admission: Adults $9, children aged 3–12 $5
Parking: Free
Phone: 352-628-5343
Website: www.homosassasprings.org

This showcase of native Florida wildlife offers visitors a rare

opportunity to observe manatees, fresh- and saltwater fish, snakes, alligators, deer, otters, and many kinds of birds in a natural setting. The huge spring at the headwaters of the Homosassa River is the centerpiece of the park, and the underwater "fishbowl" observatory allows you to see manatees and thousands of fish at close range. The park is a manatee rehabilitation center and refuge, and educational programs focus on saving and preserving these endangered mammals.

Olde Mill House Gallery and Printing Museum

Address: 10466 West Yulee Drive
Homosassa, FL 34487
Hours: Café open daily, tours of printing museum by appointment
Admission: Donation
Parking: Free
Phone: 352-628-9411

Visitors to this museum devoted to the art and craft of printing enjoy hands-on impressions as they type their names and create lead slugs on the old Linotype machine from Ybor City, then print their own cards on a small hand press under the cheerful direction of the proprietor, Jim Anderson. A printer by trade, he has assembled a remarkable collection of printing equipment from all over the state. He shares these treasures with visitors, along with the lore and history of printing, from the fifteenth-century Gutenberg press to present-day copiers. Enjoy delicious Cuban food in the café while browsing among the interesting printing artifacts.

Yulee Sugar Mill Ruins

Address: West Yulee Drive, Homosassa, FL
Mailing Address: 3400 North Museum Pointe
Crystal River, FL 34428
Parking: Free
Phone: 352-795-3817
Website: www.floridastateparks.org/yuleesugarmill

Adjacent to the Olde Mill Printing Museum in Homosassa are the imposing ruins of the sugar mill constructed by David Levy Yulee before the Civil War, now an open-air state historic site with interpretive signage. Yulee's plantation house and the sugar mill were destroyed by Federal troops who advanced up the Homosassa River after Yulee, his family, and his slaves had escaped

northward to another plantation near Archer. The massive stone chimney has been restored and the equipment used to process sugar cane has been remounted. The area is unattended, but further information is available from rangers at the Crystal River Archaeological State Park.

Brooksville

Located in the hilly ridge section of Florida, Brooksville is surrounded by the lush pastures of ranches and horse farms. A number of fine nineteenth-century homes can be seen on streets shaded by ancient oaks.

Hernando Heritage Museum

Address: 601 Museum Court
    Brooksville, FL 34601
Features: Guided tours
Hours: Tuesday–Saturday 12–3
Admission: Adults $5, children $2
Parking: Free
Phone: 352-779-0129
Website: www.hernandoheritage-museum.com

The story of Hernando County's historic past is revealed in photographs, artifacts, and clothing displayed in this late-

nineteenth-century, Victorian-style house museum. Distinctive period furnishings fill the rooms, and turn-of-the-nineteenth-century household gadgets are demonstrated by enthusiastic docents. The elegant twelve-room house with seven gables, set on spacious grounds, is embellished with gingerbread trim.

Dade City

Set among the rolling hills of Florida's heartland, this citrus growing and processing center has a strong attachment to its hometown heritage, celebrated with great zeal each September on Florida Pioneer Day.

Pioneer Florida Museum

Address: Pioneer Museum Road
    Dade City, FL 33526
Hours: Tuesday–Saturday 10–5
Admission: Adults $5, seniors $4, students age 6–18 $2,under age 6 free
Parking: Free
Phone: 352-567-0262
Website: www.pioneerfloridamuseum.org

An assemblage of artifacts and restored historic buildings offers a glimpse of the past, recalling simple virtues, hard work, and the value of craftsmanship. A church, school, railroad station, shoe shop, barn, a citrus packing house, and Cracker home have been moved to this twenty-acre park, which also has an antique train and depot on display on the grounds. Toys and dolls, Native American artifacts, vintage tools and household items,

miniature trains, and medical and dental offices with authentic equipment from yesteryear invite nostalgic browsing in the main museum building.

New Port Richey

West Pasco Historical Society Museum

Address: 6431 Circle Boulevard
New Port Richey, FL 34652
Features: Research library, picnic area nearby
Hours: Tuesday 10–1 year-round, Friday and Saturday 1–4 except during June and July
Admission: Free
Parking: Free
Phone: 727-847-0680
Website: http://www.rootsweb. com/~flwphs/

The white, wood-frame 1913 Seven Springs schoolhouse has been moved to a parklike setting overlooking a small lake, where it serves as a repository for historical materials and artifacts that tell of Pasco County's development. The old community bandstand is also on the grounds, a reminder of the boom era of the 1920s when tourists flocked to the area.

Holiday

Pasco Arts Council, Anderson House

Address: 5744 Moog Road
Holiday, FL 34690

Features: Museum shop, classes
Hours: Tuesday–Saturday 9–4
Admission: Free
Parking: Free parking behind library
Phone: 727-845-7322
Website: www.pascoart.org

111

The Anderson House, built in 1938, is the home of the Pasco Arts Council, one component of a cultural enclave located in the Holiday Centennial Park. In addition to exhibits that feature traveling shows and the works of regional artists, professional artists at the center teach classes and workshops in a variety of media. The historic 1882 Baker house, a fine example of Florida vernacular architecture, is on an adjacent site.

Tarpon Springs

Wealthy northerners built elegant homes along Spring Bayou in this winter resort before the turn of the nineteenth century. A few saw the possibilities of a sponge industry and brought experienced divers from Greece to Tarpon Springs in 1905. Today at least a third of the townspeople share a proud Greek ancestry and cultural heritage, a strong religious faith centered on the magnificent St. Nicholas Greek Orthodox Cathedral, and a tradition of good food and warm hospitality.

Tarpon Springs Cultural Center

Address: 101 South Pinellas Avenue (US 19A)
Tarpon Springs, FL 34689
Features: Museum shop
Hours: Monday–Friday 9–4, Saturday 12–4

Admission: Free
Parking: Free
Phone: 727-942-5605
Website: www.ci.tarpon-springs.
fl.us/cultural_center.htm

The 1914 red-brick City Hall with the distinctive clock tower has been restored and turned into a lively place where anything can happen—a guitar recital, a dance rehearsal, a film series, a puppet workshop, or a seminar on Greek culture. An eighty-four-seat theater is the main performance space, and the gallery exhibits are related to the arts, culture, and history of Tarpon Springs.

Tarpon Springs Historical Society Museum

Address: 160 Tarpon Avenue
Tarpon Springs, FL 34689
Hours: Tuesday–Saturday 11–4
Admission: Free
Parking: Free
Phone: 727-943-4624
Website: http://tarponspringsarea-
historicalsociety.org
E-mail: tarpon.historical@verizon.
net

In the heart of restored downtown Tarpon Springs, surrounded by antique shops and intriguing restaurants, the sturdy brick railroad station built in 1909 has become a historical museum. Artifacts, photos, and exhibits tell the story of Tarpons Springs history, and programs and events bring the city's heritage to life.

Inness Paintings, Unitarian Universalist Church

Address: 230 Grand Boulevard
Tarpon Springs, FL 34689
Mailing address: 57 Read Street,
Tarpon Springs, FL 34689
Features: Guided tours
Hours: Tuesday–Sunday 2–5; No-
vember–April, Tuesday–Sat-
urday 1–4
Admission: $1 donation
Parking: Free
Phone: 727-937-4682

Eleven large, impressionistic paintings by George Inness Jr., son of the famous American landscape artist George Inness Sr., may be viewed in the Universalist Church. The first church organized in Tarpon Springs, it is located in the historic Spring Bayou neighborhood. Inness had a home nearby, and he and his father painted many scenes of Tarpon Springs and its unspoiled natural beauty between the 1890s and 1920s.

Dunedin

This suncoast village was founded by Scottish settlers in 1870. In early spring, at the height of the winter season, Dunedin hosts its spirited Highlands Games and even incorporates bagpipers into its high school band.

113

Dunedin Fine Art Center

Address: 1143 Michigan
Boulevard
Dunedin, FL 34698
Features: Museum shop, classes,
café
Hours: Monday–Friday 10–5, Sat-
urday 10–2, Sunday 1–4
Admission: Free
Parking: Free
Phone: 727-298-3322
Website: www.dfac.org

This modern visual arts complex
has bright and airy gallery space
and features exhibits of the works
of emerging and experienced
artists. Classes and workshops
are scheduled year-round for both
beginning and seasoned artists.

Dunedin Historical Museum

Address: 349 Main Street
Dunedin, FL 34698
Features: Museum shop, research
library
Hours: Tuesday–Saturday 10–4
Admission: Adults $2 donation
Parking: Free
Phone: 727-736-1176
Website: www.dunedinmuseum.
org

Many Florida communities have

recycled their railroad stations into
museums, adapting the centrally
located buildings with their rich
historical associations to fresh
new uses. The red-brick depot in
the middle of Dunedin serves this
purpose admirably, displaying
photos, memorabilia, and exhibits
that tell the story of the town and
its environs. Railroad buffs will
enjoy the model railroad display.
In addition to the railroad station,
the Dunedin Historical Society
manages the lovely Victorian St.
Andrews Memorial Chapel located
in nearby Hammock Park. Inquire
about seasonal hours when the
chapel is open.

Safety Harbor

This community on Tampa Bay
enjoyed a heyday as a health resort
in the early part of the twentieth
century, thanks to curative springs
in the area. The homesite of Odet
Philippe, a French count and
one of the area's first settlers (in
the 1830s), has been preserved
as scenic Philippe Park on the
shores of Old Tampa Bay a few
miles north of Safety Harbor. It's
a wonderful place for a leisurely
waterfront picnic.

Safety Harbor Museum
of Regional History

Address: 329 Bayshore Boulevard
South
Safety Harbor, FL 34695
Hours: Tuesday–Friday 10–4, Sat-
urday and Sunday 1–4
Admission: Adults $3, seniors and
children under age 12 $2
Parking: Free

Phone: 727-726-1668
Website: www.safetyharbormu-
seum.org
E-mail: info@safetyharbormuseum.
org

Located in an area of placid
surroundings overlooking Tampa
Bay, the museum rests on a former
Tocobaga shell mound under a
canopy of oak and palm trees.
The grounds are an archaeological
site and various excavations have
yielded artifacts from prehistoric
Indians, the Spanish Contact, the
Civil War, and twentieth-century
Safety Harbor. The Prehistoric
Gallery includes over twelve
thousand years of history. Exhibits
trace Florida's history from the
Paleo Period, with the fossilized
remains of mastodons, mammoths,
and giant ground sloths, along
with tools that the first human
inhabitants used to hunt them. The
Heritage Gallery is dedicated to the
area's pioneers.

Largo

Close to the beaches and Tampa
Bay, this residential community
south of Clearwater shares the fine
weather and easygoing lifestyle that
attracts so many to Florida's Gulf
Coast.

Gulf Coast Museum of Art

Address: 12211 Walsingham Road
Largo, FL 33778
Hours: Tuesday–Saturday 10–4,
Sunday 12–4
Admission: Adults $8, seniors $7,
students and children aged 7–
18 $4
Parking: Free

Phone: 727-518-6833
Website: www.gulfcoastmuseum.
org

This regional complex is an
institution for visual arts collecting,
exhibiting, and teaching.
Contemporary works by Florida
and regional artists are presented
with style and imagination in eight
galleries. The extensive grounds
serve as a sculpture garden, with
many exciting works on view.
Visitors can meander and watch
the action in the individual studios
where potters, sculptors, and
painters work in an atmosphere of
creative vitality.

Heritage Village

Address: 11909 125th Street
North Largo, FL 33774
Features: Museum shop, native
plant trail, archives, reference
library
Hours: Tuesday–Saturday 10–4,
Sunday 1–4
Admission: Free
Parking: Free
Phone: 727-582-2123
Website: www.pinellascounty.
org/heritage

Plan to spend several hours
rambling around this engaging
collection of more than twenty-
five restored historic buildings
to capture a nostalgic flavor

not found in theme park "Main Streets." The outdoor living history village has brick walkways, gracious guides attired in period dress, a schoolhouse, a train depot, a boat works, a church, a store, and a variety of homes—from a log cabin to a well-furnished Victorian mansion. This is a growing institution: historic Pinellas County buildings are added from time to time as they become available, thus preserving the area's architectural heritage. Classes in pioneer crafts are scheduled and special events, such as the Pinellas Folk Festival and the Florida African American Heritage Celebration, bring the past into the present.

Indian Rocks Beach

Indian Rocks Beach Historical Museum

Address: 203 4th Avenue
  Indian Rocks Beach, FL 33785
Hours: Wednesday–Saturday 10–2
Admission: Free
Parking: Free
Phone: 727-593-3861

A 1930s cottage is the cozy home of this area museum devoted to collecting, preserving, and interpreting the history of Indian Rocks. It was expanded in 1994 with an addition to the rear. Valuable photographs on display record the early days when excursion trains brought tourists to the beach; the World War II era, when part of the beach was a bombing range; and the way the Gulf beaches looked before the advent of high-rise hotels and condominiums.

St. Petersburg

This city makes the most of a splendid waterfront setting, including a prominent pier with a building in the shape of an inverted pyramid and many cultural amenities clustered around the sparkling blue bay. Famous for its sunny weather and the nearby Gulf beaches, St. Petersburg has created a hospitable climate for the arts as well.

Museum of Fine Arts

Address: 255 Beach Drive
  Northeast
  St. Petersburg, FL 33701
Features: Museum shop, guided
  tours, concerts
Hours: Tuesday–Saturday 10–5,
  Sunday 1–5
Admission: Adults $8, seniors $7,
  students aged 7–18 $4
Parking: Free
Phone: 727-896-2667
Website: www.fine-arts.org

The serene façade of this Palladian-style building invites the visitor into a classic art museum that resembles a Renaissance villa. The comprehensive art collection of more than four thousand works includes early Asian, African, Native American, and pre-Columbian art, as well as European and American works from the seventeenth through the twentieth centuries, including works by French impressionist painters. The photography collection of more than 1,200 images is one of the most respected in Florida, and the decorative arts are beautifully presented; a dramatic gallery of Steuben and other art glass is a favorite with visitors. Special exhibitions are always on view, and two interior gardens, one of which is devoted to sculpture, encourage reflection. An interactive educational gallery is part of the recent expansion of the museum, a two-story glass conservatory that joins a wing of the original building.

St. Petersburg Museum of History

Address: 335 2nd Avenue
   Northeast
   St. Petersburg, FL 33701
Features: Museum shop, lectures
Hours: Tuesday–Saturday 10–5,
   Sunday 1–5:30, Monday 12–7
Admission: Adults $6, seniors $4,
   students $3, under age 7 free
Parking: Metered parking and ad-
   jacent city parking lot
Phone: 727-894-1052
Website: www.spmoh.org

Located on the St. Petersburg waterfront at the foot of the famous pier, this museum complements its permanent collection of prehistoric and historic artifacts with imaginative changing exhibits. A walk through time introduces visitors to the city's history, and in the Flight One Gallery, a replica of a Benoist Model 14—the world's first scheduled commercial airliner, which made its initial flight between St. Petersburg and Tampa—is suspended in the glass pavilion. Baseball memorabilia associated with teams that have held spring training in the area, as well as vintage tourist brochures and souvenirs, are popular exhibits. The extensive

costume collection is imaginatively arranged so visitors can "try on" the garments. Pick up a copy of the Historic Downtown St. Petersburg Walking Tour brochure and explore the city's architectural and historical landmarks.

Salvador Dali Museum

Address: 1000 3rd Street South
   St. Petersburg, FL 33701
Features: Museum shop, guided
   tours
Hours: Monday, Tuesday,
   Wednesday 9:30–5:30,
   Thursday 9:30–8, Friday 9:30–
   6:30, Saturday 9:30–5:30,
   Sunday 12:00–5:30
Admission: Adults $15, seniors
   and military $13.50, students
   $10, children aged 5–9 $4,
   under age 4 free; Thursdays 5
   p.m.–8 p.m. admission is $5
Parking: Free
Phone: 727-823-3767
Website: www.salvadordali
   museum.org

The Dali Museum ranks as one of Florida's top attractions and is a favorite with international visitors. Over 2,400 works by the modern Spanish artist, collected by A. Reynolds Morse and his wife, Eleanor, over a period of forty-five years, comprise the permanent collection of this museum. Paintings encompass Dali's entire career through his surrealist and classic periods. Works in the collection date from 1914 to 1976, affording visitors the opportunity to view the panorama of Dali's artistic style. In adjacent galleries, changing exhibits that complement the Dali collection provide unexpected insights. Docent-led tours are very popular, and interpretive materials are available in several languages.

Great Explorations

Address: 1925 4th Street North
    St. Petersburg, FL 33704
Features: Museum shop
Hours: Monday–Saturday 10–4:30, Sunday 12–4:30
Admission: Adults $9, seniors $8
Parking: Free
Phone: 727-821-8992
Website: http://.greatexplorations.org

This marvelous hands-on museum will delight and captivate young minds. Sensory experiences, kinetic devices, challenging puzzles, and interactive art make this a special place for children to explore and one where people of all ages can stretch their mental muscles and fire their imaginations. The young and enthusiastic staff has as much fun as the visitors and keep things running smoothly.

Florida Craftsmen Gallery

Address: 501 Central Avenue
    St. Petersburg, FL 33701
Hours: Monday–Saturday 10–5:30
Admission: Free
Parking: Free

Phone: 727-821-7391
Website: www.floridacraftsmen.net

Works of more than one hundred Florida craftsmen are showcased in a spacious gallery in the newly renovated Renaissance Building. The latest in original contemporary crafts in all media are on display in a most attractive setting. Both the oldest and the newest approaches can be seen here, from works on a grand scale for serious collectors to more modest—but quite unique—pieces. Many fine traveling exhibits are developed and assembled in this gallery, the headquarters of the statewide Florida Craftsmen organization.

The Arts Center

Address: 719 Central Avenue
    St. Petersburg, FL 33701
Features: Museum shop, classes
Hours: Tuesday–Saturday 10–5
Parking: Free on-street parking
Phone: 727-822-7822
Website: http://theartscenter.org

The Arts Center offers people of all ages and diverse cultural backgrounds the opportunity to experience and participate in the arts. Over seven hundred classes in all media are offered, and five galleries feature changing exhibitions of contemporary art. A new building is due to open in 2009 with room for

additional studio classes, a glass-blowing studio, and a permanent installation of works by renowned glass artist Dale Chihuly.

Mahaffey Theater

Address: 400 1st Street South
    St. Petersburg, FL 33701
Phone: 727-892-5798; box office
    727-892-5767
Website: http://mahaffeytheater.
    com

This cultural jewel of St. Petersburg, The Progress Energy Center for the Arts Mahaffey Theater, is a magnificent 2,000-seat performing arts center. It presents concerts by outstanding companies that bring opera, drama, music, and dance to the area. The Mahaffey Theater has been newly renovated, and patrons will enjoy the breathtaking ballroom spaces and the dramatic lobby that overlooks the Tampa Bay waterfront.

American Stage Company

Address: 211 3rd Street South
    St. Petersburg, FL 33701
Phone: box office 727-823-7529,
    theater 727-823-1600
Website: www.americanstage.org

Experience live theater in this congenial facility in a historic building in downtown St.

Petersburg, the home of Tampa Bay's oldest professional company. This flourishing center for artistic expression provides high-caliber professional theater in a wide variety of formats, including children's theater. In addition to the regular season, the players also give in-the-park performances during the summer at Demens Landing waterfront park, overlooking the South Yacht Basin.

Florida Holocaust Museum

Address: 55 5th Street South
    St. Petersburg, FL 33701
Features: Museum shop, archives,
    library
Hours: Monday–Friday 10–5, Saturday and Sunday 10–5
Admission: Adults $8, seniors and college students with I.D. $7, students and tour groups $4, museum members free
Parking: free
Phone: 727-820-0100
Website: www.flholocaustmuseum.
    org

The country's fourth-largest Holocaust museum is in downtown St. Petersburg. It is dedicated to educating the public about this unprecedented destruction of human life and to promoting the lessons of tolerance, respect, and responsibility. A dramatic highlight is Auschwitz Boxcar #113 0595-5, used to

transport victims of the Nazis to the concentration camps. Photographs, historical artifacts, and testimonies reveal the personal stories, family tragedies, and suffering of the Jewish people—from the rise of Hitler, through World War II, and during the war's aftermath. Changing exhibits present important works and collections from all over the world related to the Holocaust and associated themes.

Eckerd College, Elliott Gallery

Address: 4200 54th Avenue South
St. Petersburg, FL 33733
Hours: Monday–Friday
10:30–4:30
Admission: Free
Parking: Free
Phone: 727-864-8340

The spacious campus of Eckerd College overlooks Boca Ciega Bay, south of St. Petersburg. In the Ransom Visual Arts Center is the Elliott Gallery, a space for exhibiting fine arts and a place where students and others can gather to learn more about the artists and works being shown through gallery talks and arts study groups. Adjacent to the Arts Center is the Bininger Performing Arts Center.

Gulfport

Gulfport Historical Museum

Address: 5301 28th Avenue South
Gulfport, FL 33707
Features: Research library
Hours: Monday–Friday 2–4, Saturday 10–12
Admission: Free

Parking: Free
Phone: 727-327-0505
Website: http://gulfporthistorical-museum.homestead.com

119

Built in 1912 as the Gulfport United Methodist Church, this frame vernacular building officially opened as a historical museum in 1984. Exhibits reflect life in Gulfport during the early twentieth-century, with several period rooms on display, as well as collections of toys, clothing, and tools. The museum hosts an annual Gulfport Birthday Anniversary in October to celebrate the founding of the town in 1910.

St. Petersburg Beach

Gulf Beaches Historical Museum

Address: 115 10th Avenue
Pass-a-Grille
St. Petersburg Beach, FL 33706
Features: Museum shop
Hours: Mid-May through mid-September: Friday, Saturday 10–4 Sunday 1–4; mid-September through mid-May: Thursday–Saturday 10–4 Sunday 1–4
Admission: Free
Parking: Free
Phone: 727-552-1610
Website: www.pinellascounty.org/Heritage/gulf_beach_museum.htm

At the southern tip of the Pinellas County Gulf beaches is a small museum located in the first church built on these barrier islands in 1917. Artifacts, photographs, and vintage postcards trace the rich history of the Gulf beaches from 1500 A.D. to modern times and provide nostalgic views of a more leisurely style of vacation activities and accommodations. Set off by a white picket fence, the neat garden features sea grapes and palm trees, typical of the tropical foliage used in local landscaping.

Tampa

This bustling, modern city has a Latin flavor that gives it a tempo and style all its own, thanks to the cultural diversity introduced by the Cuban workers in the cigar industry at the turn of the nineteenth century. Historic buildings and neighborhoods display a wide range of definitive examples of Tampa's architectural heritage.

Museum of Science and Industry

Address: 4801 East Fowler Avenue
    Tampa, FL 33617
Features: Museum shops, snack
    bars, films, planetarium
Hours: Monday–Friday 9–5, Sat-
    urday and Sunday 9–6
Admission: Adults $20.95, seniors
    $18.95, children aged 2–12
    $16.75
Parking: Free
Phone: 813-987-6100,
    800-995-MOSI
Website: www.mosi.org

MOSI, the Museum of Science and Industry, is the largest science center in the southeastern United States and home of the exciting, dome-shaped MOSIMAX, the only theater of its kind in Florida. Get blown away in the Gulf Coast Hurricane Room; cruise the galaxy in the Saunders

Planetarium; stroll through BioWorks Butterfly Garden; and explore the human body in The Amazing You, the environment in Our Florida, and space and beyond in Our Place in the Universe. Visitors of all ages may engage in more than 450 hands-on activities, and there is a special area for the under-five set, Kids in Charge. The newest permanent exhibit is WeatherQuest, which focuses on the science behind natural disasters. International visitors are welcomed with special materials to add to their enjoyment of the experience.

University of South Florida, Contemporary Art Museum

Address: 4202 East Fowler
    Avenue, CAM 101
    Tampa, FL 32620
Hours: Monday–Friday 10–5, Sat-
    urday 1–4
Admission: Free
Parking: $4, request permit at
    Museum Lot C
Phone: 813-974-2849
Website: http://cam.arts.usf.edu

This campus museum presents changing exhibitions of significant contemporary art from Florida, the United States, and around the world. The museum's collection includes more than five thousand artworks, with exceptional holdings in graphics and sculpture multiples by internationally acclaimed artists, many produced at USF's Graphicstudio.

Tampa Museum of Art

Interim Address: 2306 North Howard Avenue
Tampa, FL 33607
Features: films, lectures, classes
Hours: Tuesday–Saturday 10–5, Sunday 11–5, third Fridays 8 p.m.–11p.m.
Admission: Donations
Parking: Free
Phone: 813-274-8130
Website: http://www.Tampa Museum.com

In early 2008, the Tampa Museum of Arts moved to its interim facility, while the new Tampa Museum of Art is under construction in the heart of downtown Tampa. While in the interim location, the museum will showcase exhibitions with works by regional artists, offer extensive education classes, and host a series of events. Construction of the new facility began in early 2008 and it is expected to open in the fall of 2009.

Tampa Bay Performing Arts Center

Address: 1010 North MacInnes Place
Tampa, FL 33602
Features: Tours of the complex

are given on Wednesday and Saturday
Parking: Covered pedestrian bridge links the center to the Municipal Garage to the south
Phone: Box office 813-229-7827 or 800-955-1045; tours 813-222-1000
Website: http://tbpac.org

This imposing riverfront theater complex in downtown Tampa has five auditoriums: Carol Morsani Hall—large enough for the grandest production—and the more intimate Shimberg Playhouse, Jaeb Theater, Ferguson Hall and TECO Theater. Broadway shows, chamber music, opera, classical artists, ballet, theater, and daytime programs for children are part of the year-round schedule.

Tampa Theatre

Address: 711 Franklin Street Tampa, FL 33602
Parking: Free on-street parking evenings and weekends
Phone: 813-274-8981
Website: http://tampatheatre.org

Stars shine in a flamboyant Spanish courtyard as the house lights dim and ceiling lights twinkle in the sky in this ornate, restored Hispano-Moorish-style movie palace in downtown Tampa. Concerts, special events, and films, including independent and world features and Hollywood classics, are scheduled year-round in this architectural jewel, now an official Tampa city landmark. Ask for the schedule of guided tours of the theater.

Tampa Bay History Center

The new museum, scheduled to open in late 2008, is located at Cotanchobee Fort Brooke Park in downtown Tampa and is an anchor of Tampa's Riverwalk. Please phone or consult the website for further information.
Phone: 813-228-0097
Website: http://tampabayhistory center.org

The Tampa Bay History Center is designed to bring history to life. The museum tells powerful stories and exhibits rich artifacts that bring to life the twelve-thousand-year history of Tampa Bay and Florida's west coast. The region's distinctive stories have been influenced by geography, weather, wars, immigration, development, tourism, and the integration of diverse peoples. Because the region has important historical "firsts"—in exploration, cattle, citrus, and aviation—it is an important part of America's story as well. Throughout the museum, visitors can view a world class collection of Seminole materials; an unparalleled cigar industry collection; one of the finest map collections of the southern United States, dating to the 1700s; and forty thousand other artifacts from the Tampa Bay History Center Permanent Collection. Through highly engaging and interactive exhibits, visitors will find themselves immersed in the moment and transported back in time.

Henry B. Plant Museum

Address: 401 West Kennedy Boulevard
Tampa, FL 33606
Features: Museum shop, group tours
Hours: Tuesday–Saturday 10–4, Sunday 12–4
Admission: Adults $5, children $2
Parking: Free, but ask for a parking pass
Phone: 813-254-1891
Website: www.plantmuseum.com

The Tampa Bay Hotel, built by railroad magnate Henry B. Plant, shares space with the University of Tampa and the museum, which preserves the quintessential Victorian palace featuring Moorish-revival architecture and silvered minarets. Enjoy the opulent European furniture and art treasures that furnished this Gilded-Age retreat of wealthy tourists. During the Spanish-American War, Teddy Roosevelt and his Rough Riders stayed here, adding a dashing note to the resort's history. The Annual Victorian Christmas Stroll, with all of the rooms decked out in holiday splendor, has become a favorite December tradition in Tampa.

University of Tampa, Scarfone/ Hartley Gallery

Address: 310 North Boulevard
Tampa, FL 33606
Hours: Tuesday–Friday 10–4, Saturday 1–4
Admission: Free
Parking: Free
Phone: 813-253-6217

The teaching and visual art gallery for the University of Tampa is located at Bailey Art Studios on the downtown campus. Featuring original, contemporary works of regional, national, and international artists, the gallery celebrated its thirtieth anniversary in 2007.

123

Ybor City Museum

Address: 1818 East 9th Avenue
    Tampa, FL 33605
Hours: Monday–Sunday 9–5
Admission: $3 (includes tour of "La Casita"); under age 6 free
Parking: Metered spaces, free on weekends
Phone: 813-247-6323
Website: http://www.ybormuseum.org
E-mail: info@ ybormuseum.org

The story of this multiethnic enclave established in Tampa by cigar manufacturer Don Vicente Martinez Ybor is told within this yellow-brick building, formerly the Ferlita Bakery. The brick oven designed to bake the famous Cuban bread is part of the exhibit. People of other nationalities who settled in Ybor City to work in the cigar industry are also well represented. The museum is a cooperative effort of the state and local citizens who wished to preserve memories of old Ybor City. The enclosed garden plaza, reminiscent of scenes from the immigrants' homelands, links the museum/bakery to the restored cigar workers' houses. One of these houses, "La Casita," is open to the public for guided tours.

Ellenton

Gamble Plantation Historic State Park

Address: 3708 Patten Avenue (US 301)
    Ellenton, FL 34222
Features: Museum shop, guided tours, picnic area
Hours: Thursday–Monday 9–5, house tours at 9:30, 10:30, 1, 2, 3, and 4
Admission: Tours adults $5, children $3
Parking: Free
Phone: 941-723-4536
Website: http://floridastateparks.org/gambleplantation

Enjoy a guided tour of this imposing antebellum mansion near Bradenton, furnished in the style of the 1850s, when the mansion served as the elegant centerpiece of a successful sugar plantation established by Major Robert Gamble. The historic site is also preserved as a memorial to Judah P. Benjamin, the Confederate

secretary of state who is said to have found refuge here after the fall of the Confederacy. Most of the Greek revival–style mansion is constructed of brick and tabby—a form of concrete made with water, limestone, and seashells. An interpretive center provides further insights into the history of the site. Also on the grounds is the restored Patten House, a pioneer Florida farmhouse.

Bradenton

Spanish explorers are believed to have first touched Florida shores in this area when Pánfilo de Narváez landed in 1528. When Hernando de Soto arrived eleven years later, he found only one survivor of the earlier expedition. In the 1840s, homesteaders came to the area by boat to claim fertile lands on the banks of the rivers that flow into the Gulf. Today the splendid beaches, protected bays, and sparkling waters of the Gulf of Mexico draw thousands of tourists.

Manatee Village Historical Park

Address: 1404 Manatee
   Avenue East
   Bradenton, FL 34208
Features: Museum shop, picnic
   area
Hours: Monday–Friday 9–4:30,
   Sunday 1:30–4:30, closed
   Sundays during July and August
Admission: Free
Parking: Free
Phone: 941-741-4075

Visitors are transported back to a simpler time in this growing complex of restored historical buildings. Savor the past preserved as you enter the original wood-frame courthouse built in 1860; a lovely Methodist church, very popular for weddings; a two-story brick commercial building containing Wiggins' old-fashioned store; a wooden boatworks with a job in progress; and the "Cracker Gothic" Stephens House. The pathways of the tree-shaded park are paved with bricks salvaged from Manatee County city streets.

ArtCenter Manatee

Address: 209 9th Street West
   Bradenton, FL 34205
Features: Museum shop, classes,
   workshops
Hours: Monday, Friday, Saturday
   9–5; Tuesday, Wednesday,
   Thursday 9–6
Admission: Free
Parking: Free
Phone: 941-746-2862
Website: http://artcentermanatee.
   org/

Colorful painted designs set off the front façade of this modern building, the primary center of art activity in Manatee County, located in downtown Bradenton. Three galleries display the works of local, state, and nationally known artists. Professional art instruction in a variety of media is provided in the ArtCenter studios for all ages.

South Florida Museum, Bishop Planetarium, and Parker Manatee Aquarium

Address: 201 10th Street West
Bradenton, FL 34205
Features: Museum shop, planetarium
Hours: Tuesday–Saturday 10–5, Sunday 12–5; January–April and July, Monday–Saturday 10–3, Sunday 12–5
Admission: Adults $15.95, seniors $13.95, children aged 5–12 $11.95
Parking: Free
Phone: 941-746-4132
Website: http://southfloridamuseum.org
E-mail: info@southfloridamuseum.org

This comprehensive museum, which depicts every aspect of life in the region from astronomy to zoology, is located in the heart of old Bradenton, near the waterfront. Exhibits focus on the geology of Florida, prehistoric peoples, the Spanish influence, and pioneer settlers. Here you will meet Snooty, a friendly Florida manatee who has made his home in the museum since 1948. He is the official Manatee County mascot and is very happy to greet visitors in his new aquarium. Visitors will also enjoy exploring the cosmos in the Bishop Planetarium.

DeSoto National Memorial

Address: 8300 DeSoto Memorial Drive
Bradenton, FL 34209
Features: Museum shop, nature trail
Hours: Daily 9–5
Admission: Free
Parking: Free
Phone: 941-792-0458
Website: www.nps.gov/deso

125

Travel back in time to the sixteenth century, when Spanish explorers first landed in Florida. This living history park on the shores of the Manatee River commemorates Hernando de Soto's landing in 1539. National Park Service rangers dressed as Spanish soldiers of that period have set up a rustic camp near the beach, open from mid-December through Easter Sunday. The rangers delight young visitors by showing them the fine points of the crossbow, letting them try on pieces of armor, and posing for photos with them in front of their thatched shelters. Inside the interpretive center, a twenty-two-minute film recreates the drama and the hardships of de Soto's ill-fated, four-year expedition.

Manatee Community College, Fine Art Gallery and Neel Performing Arts Center

Address: 5840 26th Street West
Bradenton, FL 34207
Hours: Gallery, Monday–Friday 9–4
Admission: Gallery free
Parking: Free
Phone: Neel Performing Arts

Center 941-752-5252; Fine Art Gallery 941-752-5225

Located on the campus southwest of Bradenton, this performing arts center hosts jazz and classical concerts, theatrical performances, and community-sponsored events in the 837-seat auditorium The Art Gallery in Building 9A features exhibits of faculty and student work, and works by nationally recognized artists.

Anna Maria Island

Anna Maria Island Museum

Address: 402 Pine Avenue
    Anna Maria Island, FL 34216
Features: Museum shop
Hours: Tuesday–Saturday 10–4
    (October 1–April 30), 10–1
    (May 1–September 30)
Admission: Free
Parking: Free (Take the free trolley
    to Stop #44)
Phone: 941-778-0492
Website: http://amihs.org

The Anna Maria Historical Park includes the Museum, the City Jail, Belle Haven Cottage, and the Mangrove Walk. The museum within the complex, which is located on the northern tip of the island, reveals the history of this picturesque Gulf coast community. Maps, rare photos, and memorabilia highlight the relaxed beach vacations and fishing excursions that have drawn some families here for generations.

Sarasota

Dynamic and wealthy Chicago socialite Mrs. Potter Palmer and circus tycoon John Ringling helped shape Sarasota's early history. Following their lead, affluent visitors, cultured patrons of the arts, and a number of interesting eccentrics have been attracted to these sheltered shores and blue bay waters.

The John and Mable Ringling Museum of Art

Address: 5401 Bay Shore Road
    Sarasota, FL 34243
Features: Museum of Art Galleries,
    Cà d'Zan Mansion, Two Circus
    Museums, Historic Asolo
    Theater Museum shops, film
    series, lectures, strollers and
    wheelchairs, restaurant and café
Hours: Daily 10–5:30
Admission: Adults $19, seniors
    $16, students and active mili-
    tary $6, under age 5 free
Parking: Free
Phone: 941-359-5700
Website: www.ringling.org

The sixty-six-acre bayfront estate, created in the 1920s by John and Mable Ringling, contains four separate and distinct museums, connected by pathways winding through lush tropical vegetation.

The Ringling Museum of Art

The classic style of Florentine Renaissance architecture lends itself to this important museum of fine arts built by John and Mable Ringling in the 1920s to house the seventeenth- and eighteenth-century paintings and decorative objects they had acquired in Europe. The collection of old masters includes five world-renowned tapestry cartoons by Peter Paul Rubens and striking Medieval and Renaissance works. Paintings are hung in groups in richly appointed galleries that reflect their style and historic contexts. One wing provides space for contemporary works and changing exhibits. Children seem to especially enjoy the spacious courtyard with its company of classical statuary.

Cà d'Zan

John Ringling named his Venetian palazzo on Sarasota Bay Cà d'Zan, which means "House of John," an exuberant showplace with touches of whimsy and playfulness, as befitted the owner of "the greatest show on earth." The extravagantly embellished exterior is matched by the splendor of the interior furnishings, carved and painted ceilings, Venetian glass windows, and marble floors. There is even a landing for his yacht and the gondolas Ringling provided for his guests. This grand palace has been recently restored to its 1920s appearance.

Circus Museum and Tibbals Learning Center

The great circus parade wagons and calliopes that brought the glamour and music of the circus right down Main Street all over the country are part of this fascinating museum of historic circus memorabilia. Also on display are dazzling costumes, clown getups and props, colorful posters, rare prints, photographs of talented circus stars of the past, and the "world's largest miniature circus."

127

Historic Asolo Theater

America's only eighteenth-century European Theater, rebuilt in the beautiful new John M. McKay Visitors Pavilion at the Ringling Estate, features a diverse roster of programming, including film, lectures, music, dance, and more.

Florida State University Center for the Performing Arts, Asolo Repertory Theater

Address: 5555 North Tamiami Trail (US 41) Sarasota, FL 34243
Parking: Free in Ringling Estate parking lot
Phone: 941-351-9010, ext. 4800
Website: www.asolo.org

Asolo Repertory Theatre is one of Florida's premiere professional

theatres. Asolo Rep originated fifty years ago in the Historic Asolo Theater at the Ringling. However, these days it performs primarily in the elegant five-hundred-seat Mertz Theatre, a lovingly restored Scottish opera house much in the same style as the Historic Asolo. The Center is home to the professional Asolo Repertory Theatre, the FSU/Asolo Conservatory for Actor Training, and the Sarasota Ballet of Florida. Additionally, students of the Conservatory perform their plays in the Cook Theater, a cozy 161-seat theater also housed in the Center.

Ringling College of Art and Design, Selby Gallery

Address: 2700 North
    Tamiami Trail (US 41)
    Sarasota, FL 34234
Hours: Monday–Saturday 10–4,
    Tuesday 10–7. Closed December 15–January 4
Admission: Free
Parking: Free
Phone: 941-359-7563
Website: www.ringling.edu
E-mail:selby@ringling.edu

Selby Gallery at the Ringling College of Art and Design is a modern showcase gallery featuring exhibitions of nationally and internationally known contemporary artists and designers. In addition, it coordinates speaking engagements and symposia with artists, designers, and educators. There are also two other galleries on the Ringling campus: Crossley Gallery, dedicated to student exhibits, and the Goldstein Gallery, dedicated to alumni exhibits.

Gulf Coast Wonder and Imagination Zone (G.WIZ)

Address: 1001 Boulevard
    of the Arts
    Sarasota, FL 34236
Features: Museum shop, classes
Hours: Monday–Friday 10–5,
    Saturday 10–6, Sunday 12–6
Admission: Adults $9, seniors $8,
    children 3–18 $6, under 3 free
Parking: Free
Phone: 941-309-4949
Website: http://gwiz.org
A tantalizing selection of hands-on experiences and discoveries awaits the visitor to this stimulating science center. There are eighty-five exciting exhibits and an Eco Zone with live snakes and turtles.

Van Wezel Performing Arts Hall

Address: 777 North Tamiami Trail
    (US 41)
    Sarasota, FL 34236
Phone: 941-955-7676,
    800-826-9303
Website: www.vanwezel.org

You can't miss this treasured architectural landmark on the bay, painted an eye-catching purple and much appreciated for its excellent acoustical and visual properties. It is a delightful place to enjoy a chamber music concert, as

well as opera, jazz, symphony, and choral productions. "Something for Everyone" programs feature Broadway musicals, pop and country music, and dance performances.

Art Center Sarasota

Address: 707 North Tamiami Trail (US 41)
    Sarasota, FL 34236
Features: Workshops, classes
Hours: Tuesday–Saturday 10–4
Admission: Donation $3
Parking: Free
Phone: 941-365-2032
Website: http://artsarasota.org

Step into the world of Florida art at this center founded in the 1920s. The patio gallery, once open to the sky in homage to the promise of perfect weather, is now enclosed and has been enlarged. First-class exhibitions feature contemporary art, with an emphasis on this Gulf coast area, which has long attracted serious and respected artists, and the sculpture garden brings art out in the open in a tropical landscape. Classes for adults and children are taught by professional instructors.

Sarasota Opera House

Address: 61 North Pineapple Avenue
    Sarasota, FL 34236
Phone: 941-366-8450
Website: www. sarasotaopera.org
E-mail: info@sarasotaopera.org

Four full-length operas are presented annually in this beautifully restored

Mediterranean-revival jewel, built in 1926. The Opera House auditorium, famous for its acoustics, seats more than one thousand people, and the lobby welcomes patrons with a dramatic grand atrium and skylight. This refined, peach-colored, three-story building has an adjacent education wing, garden courtyard, and pavilion, the latter housing the Jonas Kamlet Library of the Sarasota Opera.

Florida Studio Theater

Address: 1241 North Palm Avenue
    Sarasota, FL 34236
Phone: 941-366-9000
Website: http://fst2000.org

Housed in an intimate, historic building in Sarasota's Theater and Arts District, this professional theater presents contemporary plays and musicals on the main stage, the Gompertz Theater, and the Cabaret Stage next door.

Marie Selby Botanical Gardens

Address: 811 South Palm Avenue
    Sarasota, FL 34236
Features: Museum shops, plant shop, classes
Hours: Daily 10–5
Admission: Adults $12, children aged 6–11 $6, under age 6 free
Parking: Free
Phone: 941-366-5731
Website: www.selby.org
E-mail:contactus@selby.org

Horticultural buffs and anyone else who delights in nature's wonders must visit the Selby Gardens, a tranquil, nine-acre "supernova in the constellation of botanical gardens" overlooking Sarasota Bay. This horticultural showplace encompasses more than twenty thousand greenhouse plants. A spectacular Display Greenhouse replicates a miniature rainforest highlighted by exquisite orchids, colorful bromeliads, and other tropical plants. In addition to the alluring botanical features, waterfalls, ponds, and display gardens, the Selby House and Christy Payne Mansion have great appeal for visitors. Learn more about horticultural subjects and the history of gardens in the museum located in the mansion, or enjoy concerts and theatrical performances in the gardens on special occasions. Research in tropical horticulture is an important part of the mission of the Selby Gardens, and avid gardeners may sign up for classes and special tours.

Osprey

Historic Spanish Point

Address: 500 North Tamiami Trail
(US 41)
Osprey, FL 34229
Features: Nature trails, picnic area
Hours: Monday–Saturday 9–5,
Sunday 12–5; no tickets sold
after 4
Admission: Adults $9, residents
and seniors $8, children aged
6–12 $3
Parking: Free
Phone: 941-966-5214
Website: http://historicspanish
point.org
E-mail: info@historicspanishpoint.
org

Occupied as long ago as four thousand years by prehistoric Native Americans, this quiet oasis on Little Sarasota Bay was settled by the Webb family from New York in 1867. The shell middens left by the prehistoric Native Americans and the pioneer dwellings of the Webbs were preserved when Chicago socialite Mrs. Bertha Palmer chose the site in 1911 for her winter estate, Osprey Point. These three historical eras are interpreted in the thirty-acre tropical park, rich in native and exotic plant life, much of it introduced as part of Mrs. Palmer's formal gardens. The visitor center in the 1920s Osprey School features video presentations and changing exhibits.

6. Southwest Florida

Fort Myers

Naples

Boca Grande

Boca Grande Lighthouse Museum

Address: P. O. Box 1150
    Boca Grande, FL 33921
Features: Museum shop, fishing,
    shelling, picnic area, beach
    access
Hours: Daily 10–4 June–October
Admission: Adults $2, under age
    12 free
Parking: $2 per vehicle
Phone: 941-964-0375
Website: www.floridastateparks.
    org/gasparillaisland/

The Boca Grande Lighthouse,
built in 1890 on the southern
tip of Gasparilla Island, is one
of two functioning lights that
guard shipping on this narrow
barrier island at the mouth of
Charlotte Harbor. One room
in the lighthouse museum will
particularly delight children with
touch tables and activities devoted
to marine creatures. Other exhibits
tell the story of Gasparilla Island
from the days of the Calusa
Indians to the beginnings of the
town of Boca Grande and the
world-famous tarpon fishing
that still draws avid sportsmen
to the elegant island resort. The
restored lighthouse is part of the
127-acre Gasparilla Island State
Park. To learn even more about
the fascinating history of the
island, check out the Boca Grande

Historical Society Museum on the corner of Park and Banyan Streets and Whidden's Marina at the end of Harbor Street for a unique maritime history experience.

Punta Gorda

Visual Arts Center

Address: 210 Maude Street
   Punta Gorda, FL 33950
Features: Museum shop, classes
Hours: Monday–Friday 9–4,
   Saturday 10–2 (September–
   May), Monday–Friday 10–2
   (June–August)
Admission: Free
Parking: Free
Phone: 941-639-8810
Website: visualartscenter.com
E-mail: vac@daystar.net

Natural light and a happy spirit pervade this spacious building devoted to the visual arts. Several large galleries and wide hallways display traveling exhibits and the works of area artists. The Charlotte County Art Guild also organizes instructional classes, programs, workshops, and art demonstrations in a wide range of media.

Fort Myers

Fort Myers evolved from a frontier outpost to a bustling winter resort over the years and offers glimpses of both lifestyles to those who come to enjoy its balmy climate and casual ambiance.

Edison/Ford Winter Estates

Address: 2350 McGregor
   Boulevard
   Fort Myers, FL 33901
Features: Museum shop, garden
   shop, guided tours
Hours: Daily 9–5:30
Admission: Varies
Parking: Free
Phone: 239-334-7419
Website: www.edison-ford-estate.
   com

Thomas Edison came to Fort Myers for his health in the 1880s, at age thirty-eight. He returned each winter, living and working in the warm tropical climate until his death at age eighty-four. This most prolific of American inventors set up a chemical laboratory to conduct experiments in the production of synthetic rubber. Visit the lab, just as he left it, and the museum exhibiting many of his inventions. Edison also established an extraordinary tropical botanical garden and had a comfortable frame house—one of the country's first prefabricated houses—shipped from New England and reassembled on his fourteen-acre waterfront estate. In 1916, his good friend Henry Ford purchased the home next door, which is included in the tour.

Special in-depth historical and botanical tours can be arranged for those who want to know more about these two neighbors.

Southwest Florida Museum of History

Address: 2300 Peck Street
    Fort Myers, FL 33901
Features: Museum shop, walking
    tours, research library
Hours: Tuesday–Saturday 10–5
Admission: Adults $9.50, seniors
    $8.50, students $5
Parking: Free
Phone: 941-332-5955
Website: http://www.cityftmyers.
    com/museum

The Mediterranean-style train station just south of the historic downtown district is an exciting museum reflecting in its collections and exhibits the ebb and flow of history in this coastal region. From the era of the native Calusa people to the days of aviation training fields in World War II is a span of many centuries. A model of cattle baron Jacob Summerlin's house illuminates the rugged pioneer life, while the elegant parlor car Esperanza gives a glimpse into the Golden Age of railroad travel. Winter residents Henry Ford and Thomas Edison helped usher in the modern age, and their part in local history is also noted. In addition to an annual traveling exhibit, the museum also offers escorted day trips to other cultural and historical sites around south Florida December through April and downtown walking tours of Fort Myers January through April every Wednesday, where people will learn about the legends and lore that built Fort Myers.

Imaginarium Hands-On Museum and Aquarium

Address: 2000 Cranford Avenue
    Fort Myers, FL 33916
Features: Museum shop, café
Hours: Monday–Saturday 10–5,
    Sunday 12–5
Admission: Adults $8, seniors $7,
    children aged 3–12 $5
Parking: Free
Phone: 239-337-3332
Website: http://www.cityftmyers.
    com/imaginarium

The Imaginarium offers hands-on fun for all. Enjoy live animal encounters, dig up a dinosaur, get blown away in the Hurricane Experience, forecast the weather for WIMG-TV, play a little Bernoulli ball, shop 'til you drop in the Sweetbay Supermarket exhibit area, put on a puppet show, and have a ball exploring energy and motion! More than fifty interactive exhibits and in- and out-door exhibits and displays provide hours of fun! Three "SEA-to-SEE" Touch Tanks feature a variety of sea animals including mollusks, urchins, starfish and crabs.

William R. Frizzell Cultural Centre

Address: 10091 McGregor Boulevard
Fort Myers, FL 33919
Hours: Monday–Friday 9–5, Saturday 10–3
Admission: Free
Parking: Free
Phone: 239-939-2787
Website: http://artinlee.org
E-mail:arts@artinlee.org

The Lee County Alliance for the Arts provides enrichment and artistic enhancement in the visual arts, dance, music, and theater in this contemporary-style cultural center, which also includes the two-hundred-seat Foulds Theatre and an outdoor amphitheater. The exhibition gallery is modern and well-lighted and is host to a variety of changing shows. Many art and community events and cultural festivals are held on the spacious grounds.

Edison College, Bob Rauschenberg Gallery

Address: 8099 College Parkway Southwest
Fort Myers, FL 33919
Hours: Monday–Friday 10–4, Saturday 11–3
Admission: Free
Parking: Free
Phone: 239-489-9313

Website: www.bobrauschenberg gallery.com

The Rauschenberg Gallery on the Lee Campus of Edison College organizes seven exhibitions annually that feature artists with national and international reputations as well as notable artists of Florida.

Sanibel

Sanibel and Captiva, offshore islands connected to Fort Myers by bridges, are heaven for those who seek seashells, sunsets, and soft sand beaches. The sheltered waters of the Caloosahatchee River between these islands and the mainland have attracted people for centuries, as shown in the rich archaeological finds in the area.

Sanibel Historical Village

Address: 950 Dunlop Road
Sanibel, FL 33957
Features: Museum store
Hours: Wednesday-Saturday 10–4 (October 27–April 30)
Wednesday–Saturday 10–1 (May 1–August 11)
Admission: $5 donation
Parking: Free
Phone: 239-472-4648
Website: http://sanibelmusuem.org

To discover what life was like on Sanibel before it was linked by a bridge to the mainland and before air-conditioning, visit this airy collection of vintage wood-frame buildings, as evocative in their way as the shells that wash up on the beaches. Several cottages, Bailey's General Store, Miss Charlotte's

Tearoom, and a post office are open to the sun and breeze, simply furnished, and painted a cool white on the outside. The heritage garden is planted with the flowers, fruits, and vegetables that the pioneers grew, and the shelves of Bailey's store are still stocked with the varieties of staples for which the early twentieth-century housewife shopped.

Bailey-Matthews Shell Museum

Address: 3075 Sanibel-Captiva Road
Sanibel, FL 33957
Features: Museum shop
Hours: Daily 10–5
Admission: Adults $7, children aged 5–16 $4, under age 4 free
Parking: Free
Phone: 239-395-2233
Website: www.shellmuseum.org

Shells are gifts from the sea, and for decades the island of Sanibel has enjoyed the reputation of having one of the finest shelling beaches in the world. This beautiful museum will satisfy the most ardent shell seeker and inspire others to take up the hobby of collecting shells, if only for their beauty. But there is more to shells than beauty, as visitors will learn in the Great Hall of Shells, where specimens from all over the world are displayed and the centuries-old lore of shells is revealed. An ingenious shell identification wheel will help novices "name that shell." In a special room for children, live shell-bearing animals go quietly about their business in a shallow pool, laying eggs, grazing on sea grasses, and building their shells. Lectures and slide shows cover a wide range of shell-related topics, from fossils to endangered mollusk species.

Bokeelia

Museum of the Islands

Address: 5728 Sesame Drive Bokeelia, FL 33922
Features: Museum shop
Hours: Tuesday–Saturday 11–3, Sunday 1–4 (November1–April 30); Tuesday, Thursday, Saturday 11–3 (May 1–October 31)
Admission: Adults $2, children $1
Parking: Free
Phone: 239-283-1525
Website: http://museumof theislands.com

Venture out to Pine Island, a very lightly developed island west of Cape Coral, to get a feel for what life might have been like for the earlier inhabitants of this area, the native Calusa and the early settlers. This small, off-the-beaten-track museum proudly celebrates this heritage with exhibits of artifacts, old photographs, and items donated by pioneer families. Shell mounds on the island left behind by the Calusa are still being studied by archaeologists to learn more about this rich culture that flourished before the arrival of the Spanish.

Estero

Koreshan Historic State Park

Address: US 41 at Corkscrew Road
Mailing address: P.O. Box 7 Estero, FL 33928
Features: Guided tours, nature trail, camping, picnic area, canoe rentals, boat ramp
Hours: Daily 8-sundown; tour schedule is posted
Admission: $4 per vehicle (up to 8 passengers); guided tours, adults $2, children $1
Parking: Free
Phone: 239-992-0311
Website: http://floridastateparks. org/koreshan

One of Florida's most remarkable settlements was established on the banks of the Estero River in the 1890s. A religious visionary named Cyrus Teed brought his followers from Chicago to the wilderness to establish a "New Jerusalem." Teed's unusual theory of the universe (that the earth was a hollow sphere with the sun at the center) and the lifestyle he advocated (communal living and the practice of celibacy) doomed the experiment, but not before a great deal of creative energy was put into the settlement. Tropical gardens surround the remaining buildings, which include workshops, a bakery, several residences, and the Art Hall. Park rangers conduct tours, and

a camping area and boat ramp are available on the Estero River, which is a designated canoe trail.

Naples

Neapolitans are enthusiastic patrons of the performing and visual arts, supporting numerous art galleries and music and drama events. Historic Olde Naples, settled in the 1890s, is now a cluster of pastel-painted restored buildings and a fashionable retail center. Nearby is the Naples Pier, an important historical landmark of this Gulf coast community.

The Philharmonic Center for the Arts

Address: 5833 Pelican Bay Boulevard
Naples, FL 34108
Features: Museum shop, guided tours October–May
Hours: Monday–Friday 10–4 (October–May)
Admission: Galleries adults $4, students $2
Parking: Free
Phone: 239-597-1900 or 800-597-1900
Website: http://thephil.org
E-mail: info@thephil.org

This resplendent cultural showplace, called The Phil, has a 1,425-seat concert hall and a more intimate theater that seats two hundred for chamber music, jazz, and lecture programs in the arts and humanities. Galleries exhibit changing art shows, and the center's permanent collection of sculpture enlivens the elegant lobby and open-air sculpture garden. A parapet spiked with spires adds a festive note to the roofline of this engaging building, an architectural celebration of the arts.

Palm Cottage

Address: 137 12th Avenue South
    Naples, FL 34102
Hours: Tuesday–Saturday
    1–4 (November–April),
    Wednesday and Saturday 1–4
    (May–October)
Admission: Adults $6, under age
    12 $3
Parking: Metered on-street spaces
Phone: 239-261-8164
Website: http://napleshistorical
    society.org

One of the oldest homes in Naples is now the headquarters of the Naples Historical Society. Built in 1895 and located one block east of the Naples Pier, this simple, one-story house is set off with a white picket fence and furnished with period antiques. Ask about guided walking tours of the Naples Historic District.

Collier County Museum

Address: 3301 Tamiami Trail East
    Naples, FL 34102
Features: Museum shop, research
    library, picnic area
Hours: Monday-Friday 9–5, Sat-
    urday 9–4
Admission: Free
Parking: Free
Phone: 239-774-8476
Website: http://colliermuseum.com

The broad sweep of more than ten thousand years of history

is presented in this museum complex. In the permanent exhibit hall, fossils and artifacts of long-vanished Native American civilizations—as well as those of Seminoles, pioneers, and early settlers—trace the history of Collier County from prehistoric time to the present. A homesteader's cottage and a vintage logging locomotive are also on the grounds.

Chokoloskee

Historic Smallwood Store Museum

Address: 360 Mamie Street or P.O.
    Box 367
    Chokoloskee, FL 34138
Hours: Daily 10–5 (December 1–
    May 1), Friday–Tuesday 10–4
    (May 2–November 30)
Admission: Donation
Parking: Free
Phone: 239-695-2989

Pioneer storekeeper and postmaster Ted Smallwood built his trading post high on pilings in the edge-of-the-Everglades hamlet of Chokoloskee, south of Naples, in 1906. Seminoles came by canoe to trade. A handful of hardy settlers, mostly fishermen and hunters, also came by boat until a road to the island community was completed in the 1950s. Visitors will find a fascinating slice of Old Florida history as they browse through the store, its open shelves still stocked with the goods essential to life in this tiny, remote fishing village.

7.

Southeast Florida

Stuart

Palm Beach

Fort Lauderdale

Miami

Stuart

This coastal enclave of posh condominiums and regal retirement communities has an active Council for the Arts to coordinate visual and performing arts programs. Downtown Stuart is rich in historic architecture, reflecting its settlement over one hundred years ago. Follow A1A, the coastal highway, to Hutchinson Island, a narrow sliver of land between the Indian River and the Atlantic Ocean.

Stuart Heritage Museum

Address: 161 Southwest Flagler
    Avenue
    Stuart, FL 34994
Hours: Monday–Saturday 10–3
Admission: Free
Parking: Free
Phone: 772-220-4600

The two-story, red-painted general store once operated by George Parks is now the local history museum, a charming and inviting emporium of memories. Pioneering families are honored and the heritage of the past is presented in dioramas of Stuart's turn-of-the-last-century business area, clothing, tools used by pineapple growers and fishermen, and a myriad of items that Mr. Parks might have offered his customers. Historic walking tour brochures are available for those who enjoy exploring local architecture, which ranges from a 1920s movie theater to "Millionaire's Row."

Court House Cultural Center

Address: 80 East Ocean Boulevard
   Stuart, FL 34994
Hours: Monday–Friday 10–4
Admission: Free
Parking: Free
Phone: 772-287-6676

The 1930s art deco–style Martin
County courthouse now presents a
changing program of visual arts in
its first-floor galleries. Located in
the heart of revitalized downtown
Stuart, the restored historical
building is the hub of cultural
activities for the community.

Florida Oceanographic Coastal Center

Address: 890 Northeast Ocean
   Boulevard
   Stuart, FL 34996
Features: Museum shop, nature
   trails
Hours: Monday–Saturday 10–5,
   Sunday 12–4
Admission: Adults $8, children
   aged 3-12 $4
Parking: Free
Phone: 772-225-0505
Website: http://floridaocean
   ographic.org/

Enthusiastic docents greet visitors
and introduce them to fascinating
coastal flora and fauna—including
live specimens in touch tanks,
where you can pet and feed the
stingrays. Check out the Game
Fish Lagoon and inspect the
aquariums. Stroll down to the
Indian River on the boardwalk
through oak hammocks and
mangrove marshes, a real delight
to bird watchers and nature
photographers.

Elliott Museum

Mailing address: 825 Northeast
   Ocean Boulevard
   Stuart, FL 34996
Features: Museum shop, picnic
   area and beach access in adja-
   cent park
Hours: Monday–Saturday 10–4,
   Sunday 1–4
Admission: Adults $7, children
   aged 6–13 $2, under age 6 free
Parking: Free
Phone: 772-225-1961
Website: http://elliottmuseumfl.org

The Elliott Museum, built in 1961
in honor of the prolific inventor
Sterling Elliott, houses an array of
exhibits including art, antiques,
textiles and automobiles. The
museum also presents the history
of Martin County, from the
fossilized bones of the animals
that roamed the area ten thousand
years ago to the artifacts from
families that settled here. Take a
stroll down memory lane in the
Americana wing, which features
several nostalgic displays, as
well as exhibits dedicated to the
inventions and innovation of both
Sterling and Harmon Elliott. The
Car Gallery features over thirty-
five antique automobiles and
motorcycles, from a 1903 Cadillac
Runabout to a mint condition
1957 Chevy Bel-Air convertible.

House of Refuge Museum at Gilbert's Bar

Physical Address: 301 Southeast
   MacArthur Boulevard
   Stuart, FL 34996
Mailing address: 825 Northeast
   Ocean Boulevard
   Stuart, FL 34996

Features: Museum shop, picnic area, beach access
Hours: Monday–Saturday 10–4, Sunday 1–4
Admission: Adults $5, children aged 6–13 $2, under age 6 free
Phone: 772-225-1875
Website: http://www.houseof refugefl.org/houseofrefuge/index.html

Florida's often stormy shores were once dotted with houses of refuge, built along the barren east coast of Florida in the late 1800s as havens for shipwrecked sailors and travelers. This last remaining station, built in 1876, is located on Hutchinson Island and sits perched on a high ridge between the Atlantic Ocean and the Indian River overlooking the St. Lucie Rocks, a particularly rugged Atlantic coast shoreline. The House of Refuge at Gilbert's Bar displays navigation and rescue equipment and documents the work of the U.S. Lifesaving Service. It provides a look at turn-of-the-nineteenth-century living along the coast as visitors may view the Keeper's quarters featuring a kitchen, dining room, parlor, and bedroom. Exhibit space in the lower level includes Indian artifacts from Hutchinson Island's earliest inhabitants.

Maritime and Yachting Museum

Address: 3250 Southwest Kanner Highway
Stuart, FL 34994
Hours: Monday–Saturday 11–4, Sunday 1–5
Admission: Adults $4, children $1
Parking: Free
Phone: 772-692-1234
Website: www.mymfllorida.com

Boating and sailing have been part of the history of this area since the days of the first settlers, who relied mostly on water transportation before the arrival of railroads and highways. Lovers of maritime memorabilia, yachting artifacts, ship's models, navigational instruments, and nautical lore will be drawn to this museum. A restoration program that preserves older vessels is part of the museum's mission.

Tequesta

Lighthouse Center for the Arts

Address: 373 Tequesta Drive
Tequesta, FL 33469
Features: Museum shop
Hours: Monday–Saturday 10–4:30
Admission: Free
Parking: Free
Phone: 561-746-3101
Website: http://lighthousearts.org

As northern Palm Beach County's oldest and largest visual arts museum, the Lighthouse Center for the Arts is a two-building operation featuring a stand-alone school of art with classes for children and adults, beginner through professional levels, and diverse and educational exhibits. Programs also include Profile Guest Lectures and the Jazz Series.

Jupiter

Jupiter Inlet Lighthouse and Museum

Address: Lighthouse Park, 500
   Captain Armours's Way
   Jupiter, FL 33469
Features: Museum shop, tours
Hours: Tuesday–Sunday 10–5
Admission: Adults $7, children
   aged 6-18 $5
Parking: Free
Phone: 561-747-8380
Website: www.lrhs.org

This familiar red sentinel was built in the 1850s to guard the entrance to Jupiter Inlet. Today, visitors may climb the steps to the top of the lighthouse for a fabulous view. The waterfront museum is in the restored World War II building in the nearby Lighthouse Park, where exhibits of maritime and pioneer life are displayed. Don't miss the historic Tindall House on the museum grounds. The Lighthouse, Museum, Tindall House, and DuBois House (across the Loxahatchee River) are all operated by the Loxahatchee River Historical Society.

DuBois Pioneer Home

Address: DuBois Park
   Jupiter, FL 33477
Hours: Tuesday and Wednesday
   1–4
Admission: $2
Parking: Free
Phone: 561-747-8380, extension
   101
Website: www.lrhs.org

Across the Loxahatchee River from the Jupiter Inlet Lighthouse is the home of pioneer Harry DuBois. He built the house in 1887 on a shell mound, the site of a pre-Columbian village, for his new bride. The structure, which has survived many hurricanes, is a good example of early Florida vernacular architecture. Many of the family's furnishings and household objects are in place to illustrate the frontier lifestyle.

141

Florida Atlantic University, Hibel Museum of Art

Address: 5353 Parkside Drive
   FAU-John D. MacArthur
   Campus
   Jupiter, FL 33458
Features: Museum shop, concerts
Hours: Tuesday–Saturday 11–4
Admission: Free
Parking: Free
Phone: 561-622-5560
Website: http://hibelmuseum.org

A welcoming museum devoted to the works of Edna Hibel, noted American impressionist, is located on the corner of University and Main Streets across from the Roger Dean Stadium. Her prolific work, featured in the collections of many major museums, appears in a wide range of media—fresco, canvas, wood, silk, plaster, oil glaze, gold leaf, and porcelain. In addition to the drawings, paintings, sculpture, and lithography by Hibel, antique furniture and glass are displayed in the museum. Enjoy chamber music concerts by distinguished performers and elegant teas hosted by the artist herself from November through May.

Palm Beach

Extravagant shops, polo and tennis clubs, and elegant restaurants cater to the very rich and very famous, whose homes line the oceanfront drive. Many of the buildings in this American Riviera were designed in the 1920s by Addison Mizner, creator of the classic Florida look inspired by posh Mediterranean villas and estates.

The Henry M. Flagler Museum, Whitehall

Address: 1 Whitehall Way
    Palm Beach, FL 33480
Features: Museum shop, guided tours, audio tours, café
Hours: Tuesday–Saturday 10–5, Sunday 12–5
Admission: Adults $15, children 13–18 $8, children aged 6–12 $3
Parking: Free
Phone: 561-655-2833
Website: www.flaglermuseum.us

After a career as a founding partner in Standard Oil, Henry Morrison Flagler turned his interests to developing Florida. His East Coast Railroad and the luxury hotels he built along its route linked the entire Atlantic coast of Florida and made Palm Beach one of the world's great winter resorts. Whitehall, the home he built in 1902 as a wedding present, was described as "the Taj Mahal of North America." The Marble Hall entrance sets the tone for a tour of this magnificent mansion. In room after room, elegant furnishings reflect the opulence that set the

style for Florida's Gold Coast. The Rambler, Flagler's private railroad car, which was built in 1887 to his specifications, was the first train into Key West in 1912 when his Florida East Coast Line was completed. It is housed in the Flagler Pavilion, where the Museum Café is also located.

Society of the Four Arts

Address: Four Arts Plaza
    Palm Beach, FL 33480
Features: Library, lectures, films, gardens
Hours: Gallery, Monday–Saturday 10–5, Sunday 2–5 (December–April); gardens open daily 10–5
Admission: Varies
Parking: Free
Phone: 561-655-7226
Website: http://fourarts.org

Elegant surroundings and a discriminating program are features of this cultural center devoted to art, music, drama, and literature—the four arts. From November through April, art exhibits, speakers, concerts, and films are presented. In addition to

the art galleries and auditorium, located in a building designed by Addison Mizner, enjoy the beautiful botanical and sculpture gardens. A fine arts reference library is on the second floor of the Fine Arts building, and there is an enchanting children's library.

West Palm Beach

Henry Flagler established this town across Lake Worth from Palm Beach as a commercial center and residential community for the workers on his East Coast Railroad. It has a vibrant cultural life of its own and is less influenced by the seasonal fluctuation of its population than Palm Beach.

Norton Museum of Art

Address: 1451 South Olive Avenue
    West Palm Beach, FL 33401
Features: Museum shop, theater, sculpture garden, guided tours, café
Hours: Monday–Saturday 10–5, Sunday 1–5
Admission: Adults $8, young people aged 13–21 $3
Parking: Free
Phone: 561-832-5196
Website: www.norton.org

The Norton Museum of Art is one of the Southeast's premier art museums, known for the quality of its extensive collections, traveling special exhibitions, and innovative educational programming. The Norton has an internationally renowned collection of American, European, Chinese, and contemporary art, as well as photography,

143

and presents exhibition related lectures, concerts, and programs for children and adults. European Impressionists and Modern Masters, such as Georges Braque, Paul Gauguin, Henri Matisse, Claude Monet, Pablo Picasso, and Pierre Auguste Renoir are represented, and twentieth-century American artists such as Stuart Davis, Hopper, O'Keeffe, and Warhol star in the collection. The Chinese collection is one of the most notable in the United States.

Ann Norton Sculpture Gardens

Address: 253 Barcelona Road
    West Palm Beach, FL 33401
Hours: Wednesday–Sunday 11–4, closed in August
Admission: $5
Parking: Free
Phone: 561-832-5328
Website: http://ansg.org

The historic home, studio, and garden of Ann Weaver Norton, a prominent sculptor and wife of the founder of the Norton Museum of Art, form a quiet sanctuary in the heart of the Art District. A permanent installation of Mrs. Norton's monumental abstract sculptures graces the garden, where hundreds of varieties of palms and

other tropical plantings create a jungle-like ambiance. With such a backdrop, the massive works of the artist take on the appearance of mysterious ancient relics. The Norton home provides gallery space for changing exhibits in an intimate setting.

Kravis Center for the Performing Arts

Address: 701 Okeechobee
Boulevard
West Palm Beach, FL 33401
Phone: 561-832-7469
Website: http://www.kravis.org

Boldly modern in its architectural style, this multipurpose performing arts complex presents a dynamic and varied schedule of performances from classical to the cutting-edge, including ballet, pop, jazz, Broadway, opera and more. Many regionally based arts organizations call the Kravis Center their home, including Ballet Florida, Miami City Ballet, Palm Beach Opera, and the Palm Beach Pops.

Armory Art Center

Address: 1700 Parker Avenue
West Palm Beach, FL 33401

Features: Studio classes, workshops
Hours: Monday–Friday 10–4, Saturday 10–2
Admission: Donations suggested, $5
Parking: Free
Phone: 561-832-1776
Website: http://armoryart.org

The restored historic Palm Beach County National Guard Armory is a handsome art deco–style building in a parklike setting. The Armory serves as a leading visual arts center for the area, providing art education and enrichment for all ages. Professional faculty teach more than fifty studio courses during the year, and the winter Master Artists Workshop draws participants from all over the country to sunny south Florida. The Armory Gallery displays changing exhibits of the works of major artists from all over the world.

South Florida Science Museum

Address: 4801 Dreher Trail North
West Palm Beach, FL 33405
Features: Museum shop, planetarium, aquarium, picnic area
Hours: Monday–Friday 10–5, Saturday 10–6, Sunday 12–6
Admission: Adults $9, seniors $7.50, children aged 3–12 $6
Parking: Free
Phone: 561-832-1988
Website: www.sfsm.org

Children eagerly engage in both changing and permanent exhibits that invite exploration, discovery, and hands-on experiences, and their parents soon find themselves involved as well. Playing with sound, light, electrical forces, and other physical phenomena makes learning fun. An aquarium and a planetarium complement the exhibits. The museum is located in Dreher Park.

Clewiston

Ah-Tha-Thi-Ki Museum

Address: HC-61, Box 21-A
     Clewiston, FL 33440
Features: Museum store, guided
     tours, craft classes
Hours: Daily 9–5
Admission: Adults $6, seniors and
     children aged 6–17 $4,
     under age 6 free
Parking: Free
Phone: 863-902-1113
Web Site: www.ahtahthiki.com

The Seminole Tribe invites visitors to enter the Big Cypress Reservation and come to "a place to learn, a place to remember," the meaning of Ah-Tha-Thi-Ki. The museum features generous gallery space that showcases artifacts and lifelike dioramas depicting Seminole life at the turn of the last century and highlights the history, art, and culture of the Seminole Tribe of Florida. A one-mile raised boardwalk winds through a sixty-

six-acre cypress dome.

Coconut Creek

Butterfly World

Address: 3600 West
     Sample Road, Tradewinds Park
     Coconut Creek, FL 33073
Features: Museum shop, plant
     shop, classes, café, picnic area
Hours: Monday–Saturday 9–5,
     Sunday 11–5
Admission: Adults $21, children
     aged 3–11 $15
Parking: Free, but Tradewinds
     Park has a $1 gate fee on
     weekends
Phone: 954-977-4400
Website: http://butterflyworld.com
E-mail: gardens@butterflyworld.
     com

The air in the tropical garden setting is alive and sparkling with brilliantly colored butterflies, and visitors are enchanted with their fragile and exotic beauty. Learn about the miracle of metamorphosis and watch butterflies emerging from their cocoons. Different kinds of gardens have been planted to attract native butterflies; learn from experts how to plant your own backyard butterfly garden. A series of aviaries hums and flutters with hummingbirds and colorful tropical birds, and spectacular insect specimens are on display in the Live Bug Zoo. Butterfly World is located in Tradewinds Park, a huge recreation area west of Pompano Beach.

Delray Beach

Named by homesick settlers from Michigan around 1900 for a suburb in Detroit, this town experienced all the highs and lows of the Florida land boom and bust in the 1920s. It is a flourishing residential community today, with a bustling shopping and commercial district along Atlantic Avenue.

Old School Square
Cultural Arts Center

Address: 51 North Swinton
  Avenue
  Delray Beach, FL 33444
Hours: Tuesday–Saturday 10:30–
  4:30, Sunday 1–4:30 (closed
  Sundays May–September)
Admission: Adults $6, students $4,
  under age 13 free
Parking: Free
Phone: Crest Theatre Box Office
  561-243-7922 ext. 1; Cornell
  Museum 561-243-7922
Website: www.oldschool.org

In the center of town, the 1913 Mediterranean-style Delray Beach elementary and high schools have been restored and turned into a vibrant center for the visual and performing arts. The Crest Theatre presents professional theater, dance, and music, and the Cornell Museum of Art and American Culture features rotating fine arts exhibits. The 1926 gymnasium and outdoor amphitheatre provide additional gathering and performance space.

Palm Beach Photographic Center

Address: 55 Northeast Second
  Avenue
  Delray Beach, FL 33444
Features: Photo shop next door,
  workshops, classes, free lectures
Hours: Monday–Saturday 9-6
Admission: $3
Phone: 561-276-9797
Website: http://workshop.org
E-mail: cs@workshop.org

Dedicated to preservation of the art of photography and digital imaging, this center also presents a full schedule of classes, with a major week-long session, FotoFusion, scheduled at the peak of the winter season. Exhibitions change regularly in the well-lighted and spacious gallery, with the works of award-winning photographers such as Margaret Bourke-White on display. Lecture series and weekend workshops explore photography basics, innovations, professional development, and art photography.

Morikami Museum
and Japanese Gardens

Address: 4000 Morikami Park
  Road
  Delray Beach, FL 33446
Features: Museum shop, Japanese
  café, classes, research library,

nature trails, picnic area
Hours: Tuesday–Sunday 10–5
Admission: Adults $10, seniors $9,
   children aged 6–18 $6
Parking: Free
Phone: 561-495-0233
Website: http://morikami.org

Not many people know that
a colony of Japanese farmers
settled in Palm Beach County in
the early 1900s. This splendid
museum preserves and interprets
the essence of Japanese culture
as a part of Florida history, as
well as exhibiting traditional
and contemporary Japanese art
and culture. The gardens and
two-hundred-acre park were
developed on land left to the
people of Florida by George
Morikami, a leader in the Japanese
farming colony called Yamato,
near Boca Raton. This tranquil
landscape evokes a distinctive
Asian character with its fish ponds,
waterfalls, arched bridges, and
curving pathways. Visit the Bonsai
and Japanese Gardens and enjoy
seasonal festivals, tea ceremonies,
and demonstrations of such
traditional crafts as origami and
kite-making, which offer further
glimpses into Japanese culture.

Boca Raton

Architect Addison Mizner,
who designed many of the
Mediterranean-style mansions in
Palm Beach, initiated an elaborate
planned community in Boca
Raton in the 1920s, but the end
of the real estate boom halted its
completion. However, Mizner and
the elite lifestyle he represented are
still revered and honored: polo is
the local sport of choice.

Florida Atlantic University, Schmidt Center Gallery and Ritter Gallery

Address: 777 Glades Road
   Boca Raton, FL 33431
Hours: Tuesday–Friday 1–4, Sat-
   urday 1–5
Admission: Free
Parking: Park in metered spaces
Phone: 561-297-2966
Website: www.fau.edu/galleries

The spacious campus of FAU
is dotted with artificial lakes,
landscaped with flowering
hibiscus, and graced by many
large outdoor sculptures. Two art
galleries on campus, the Schmidt
Center Gallery in the College
of Arts and Humanities and the
Ritter Gallery, provide space for
changing exhibits of professional
and student works.

Boca Raton Museum of Art

Address: 501 Plaza Real
   Boca Raton, FL 33432
Features: Museum shop, guided
   tours, classes, lectures
Hours: Tuesday, Thursday, and
   Friday 10–5, Wednesday 10–9,
   Saturday and Sunday 12–5
Admission: Adults $8, seniors $5,

students $4, under age 12 free
Parking: Free
Phone: 561-392-2500
Website: http://www.boca
museum.org

A shaded sculpture garden
enhances the setting of this
growing art center. Changing
exhibitions of high quality and
a strong permanent collection
draw community support for
and interest in the museum. The
permanent collection contains
superb works by modern masters,
including Degas, Braque, de
Chirico, Klee, Picasso, and
Modigliani. Art enrichment and
aesthetic development are the aim
of an ambitious series of lectures
and classes.

Children's Museum

Address: 498 Crawford Boulevard
Boca Raton, FL 33432
Features: Museum store, picnic
area, nature trail
Hours: Tuesday–Saturday 12–4
(closed first week after the 4th
of July)
Admission: $3
Parking: Free, behind building
Phone: 561-368-6875
Website: http://cmboca.org

A charming cottage called "Singing
Pines," the oldest house in town,
welcomes little children and their
parents to play dress-up, sing and
dance, dig for fossils, read quietly,
play store, and have fun together.
Designed for kids between the
ages of four and ten, the museum
is nestled in an intimate garden
of native plants and shrubs.

The model carousel in the lobby
enchants children, and changing
activities and exhibits invite many
repeat visits.

Boca Raton Historical Society Museum

Address: 71 North Federal
Highway
Boca Raton, FL 33432
Features: Museum shop, library,
guided tours
Hours: Monday–Friday 10–4, Sat-
urday 10–2
Admission: Free
Parking: Free, behind building
Phone: 561-395-6766
Website: http://www.bocahistory.
org

The restored 1927 Boca Raton
Town Hall, with its gleaming
golden dome, is the location of this
posh local history museum. Photos
from the town archives show how
times have changed. To see the
town's historical and architectural
gems today, visitors can take
Historical Society tours of the Boca
Raton Resort (Addison Mizner's
original Cloister Inn) and narrated
trolley tours of the city.

Davie

Flamingo Gardens

Address: 3750 Flamingo Road
Davie, FL 33330
Features: Museum shop, plant
shop, guided tours
Hours: Daily 9:30–5:30 (Closed
Mondays June 1–September 30)
Admission: Adults $17, children
$8.50; additional charge for
tram tour

Parking: Free
Phone: 954-473-2955
Website: http://flamingogardens.
   org

Tropical birds and plants make this botanical garden an enchanting place to spend a few leisurely hours. There are gardens that attract butterflies and hummingbirds, aviaries alive with colorful tropical birds, and gardens and greenhouses glowing with exotic blossoms. Established in the 1920s as part of a citrus grove, the twelve-acre botanical garden contains specimen palms, orchids, ferns, bromeliads, and other rare trees and shrubs. A narrated tram tour winds through the groves and native hammock and wetlands areas.

Broward Community College, Fine Arts Gallery and Bailey Concert Hall

Address: 3501 Southwest Davie
   Road, Building 3
   Davie, FL 33314
Hours: Gallery Monday–Friday 9–
   2, Saturday 11–2
Admission: Free
Parking: Free
Phone: Gallery 954-201-6984, box
   office 954-475-6884
Website: www.broward.edu

A wall of windows facing a landscaped courtyard admits a profusion of natural light to this fine art gallery, where works of nationally recognized artists, as well as regional Florida artists and BCC students, are featured in changing exhibits. Across the courtyard is the impressive Bailey Concert Hall, which presents a spectacular schedule of concerts and performance events. The Buehler Planetarium is also located on this campus and invites the public to enter and observe the solar system.

Fort Lauderdale

Famous for its beautiful beach, posh residences, and shops, Fort Lauderdale has other charming attractions as well. An Arts and Science District has been designated in downtown Fort Lauderdale on the banks of the New River, where the original Seminole trading posts and commercial buildings were located. Enjoy the relaxing ambiance of the Riverwalk, where brick pathways follow the water's edge and festival events bring celebrations to life in the lushly landscaped parks and plazas.

Bonnet House Museum and Gardens

Address: 900 North Birch Road
   Fort Lauderdale, FL 33304
Features: Museum shop, lectures,
   programs for children
Hours: Tuesday–Saturday 10–4,
   Sunday 12–4
Admission: Adults $20, seniors
   $18, students aged 6–12 $16;
   grounds only, $10

Parking: Free
Phone: 954-563-5393
Website: www.bonnethouse.org

Surrounded by highrises, this thirty-five-acre estate near the ocean is set in a lush, subtropical landscape. The plantation-style home, designed early in the twentieth century by Chicago art collector Frederic Bartlett, takes its name from the native yellow bonnet water lilies growing in three freshwater ponds on the property. An open veranda and sheltered courtyards bring the outdoors into the bright and airy interior. One of the country's largest orchid collections further enhances the beauty of this unique house museum.

International Swimming Hall of Fame Museum

Address: 1 Hall of Fame Drive
    Fort Lauderdale, FL 33316
Features: Museum shop, library
Hours: Daily 9–5
Admission: Adults $8, seniors $6, students $4
Parking: Free
Phone: 954-462-6536
Website: www.ishof.org/museum

Olympic-quality swimmers and divers have been training in Fort Lauderdale since the 1920s, when the Casino Pool opened, and the tradition continues today at this complex with several pools, a stadium for events and swim meets, and a museum dedicated to the aquatic sports of swimming, diving, water polo, and synchronized swimming. Memories of past Olympic games and championships are captured in excellent exhibits of uniforms, medals, photos, memorabilia, and artwork.

Museum of Art | Fort Lauderdale

Address: 1 East Las Olas
    Boulevard
    Fort Lauderdale, FL 33301
Features: Museum shop, guided tours, café
Hours: Daily 11–7, closed Tuesday
Admission: Varies
Parking: Metered spaces in municipal parking garage to the east
Phone: 954-525-5500
Website: www.moafl.org

Soaring spaces and the swoop of the stairway leading to the second level draw visitors into the heart of this major art museum. There is room to move around,

room to see the individual and collected works to best advantage, and room to contemplate and appreciate the skill with which the art is presented. Major changing exhibits on the first floor feature challenging and exciting works, and there are special art spaces for younger visitors. The museum is located in Fort Lauderdale's Riverwalk Arts and Entertainment District.

Fort Lauderdale Historical Society

Address: 219 Southwest
2nd Avenue
Fort Lauderdale, FL 33301
Features: Museum shop, research library and archives, walking tours
Hours: Tuesday–Saturday 10–5, Sunday 12–5
Admission: Tours Adults $10, students $5
Parking: Metered on-street parking
Phone: 954-463-4431
Website: www.oldfortlauderdale. org

Located on the New River, this complex of historic structures tells the story of the community's history from the pioneers of Fort Lauderdale to the present day through its four historic structures: the 1905 New River Inn, which houses the Museum of History;

the 1905 Philemon Bryan House, a four-square vernacular-style house; the 1905 Acetylene Building, which produced acetylene gas to light the New River Inn; and the 1907 King-Cromartie House Museum, which belonged to one of the first pioneer families in Fort Lauderdale. The site also includes a replica of the first Broward County schoolhouse and the Hoch Heritage Center, a public research library that holds the largest collection of material related to greater Fort Lauderdale, including more than 250,000 historic photographs.

Broward Center for the Performing Arts

Address: 201 Southwest 5th
Avenue
Fort Lauderdale, FL 33312
Parking: Metered spaces in Arts and Science garage
Phone: 954-522-5334
Website: http://browardcenter.org

Facing the Esplanade Park at a graceful bend in the New River is a Mediterranean-inspired showcase for arts and entertainment with red-tile roofs and stucco walls, bright colors and shaded porches, and two separate theaters. Relax and appreciate the other welcoming amenities—such as outdoor dining patios, tropical landscaping, outdoor sculpture, a gift shop, and spectacular views of the river and the city—as you enjoy performances of Broadway shows, jazz and pop concerts, children's theater, films, lectures, and much more.

Museum of Discovery and Science

Address: 401 Southwest 2nd Street
Fort Lauderdale, FL 33312
Features: Museum shop
Hours: Monday–Saturday 10–5,
Sunday noon–6
Admission: Adults $10, seniors
$9, children aged 2–12 $8; additional charge for IMAX®
tickets
Parking: Metered parking in Arts
and Science garage
Phone: 954-467-6637
Website: www.mods.org

Spend a day of discovery with the museum's interactive exhibits and the featured traveling exhibit. You can hang out with bats, turtles, alligators, and pet a big green iguana. Fly like an astronaut and immerse yourself in a giant-screen IMAX® adventure.

Old Dillard Museum

Address: 1009 Northwest 4th
Street
Fort Lauderdale, FL 33311
Hours: Monday–Friday 11–4
Admission: Free
Parking: Free
Phone: 754-322-8828

The Old Dillard School was built in 1924 for African-American students. On the second floor of this restored educational landmark are displays that highlight the significant contributions of the African-American community to Broward County. Other exhibits and an interactive gallery focus on diverse African cultures, ethnic art, and creative experiences. The Jazz Room features the life of saxophonist Cannonball Adderley, who taught instrumental music at Dillard High School before moving to New York to join the Miles Davis sextet in 1955.

Historic Stranahan House Museum

Address: 335 Southeast 6th
Avenue
Fort Lauderdale, FL 33301
Features: Museum shop, guided
tours
Hours: Wednesday–Sunday 1–
3:30, guided tours every half
hour
Admission: Adults $12, children
$7
Phone: 954-524-4736
Website: http://stranahanhouse.
org

The oldest house in Broward County was built in 1901 as a trading post for Seminoles who paddled down the New River from their villages in the Everglades. Warmly interpreted and furnished to recreate the period from 1913 to 1915, when plumbing and electricity were added, this is one of the most delightful of Florida's house museums. The house's site on the south bank of the river—which was also the location of the ferry service Frank Stranahan provided in the bridgeless days of the early twentieth century—made it the hub of economic and social life in the frontier settlement.

Dania

International Fishing Hall of Fame

Address: 300 Gulfstream Way
Dania, FL 33004
Hours: Daily 10–6

Admission: Adults $6, seniors $5, children aged 3–16 $5
Phone: 954-783-0036
Website: www.igfa.org

A world-class museum with traditional and interactive exhibits located near the Fort Lauderdale Airport captures all the thrills of sport fishing. If you love to fish, you will enjoy the displays of fishing technology, historical artifacts, and interactive simulators that let you try for the big ones without getting wet. The IGFA has an extensive library related to sport fishing and keeps up with all of the international fishing records, in case you want to know how your catch measures up to world standards.

Hollywood

Art and Culture Center of Hollywood

Address: 1650 Harrison Street
   Hollywood, FL 33020
Features: Classes, films, lectures
Hours: Monday–Saturday 12–4
Admission: Adults $6, seniors and students $3, under age 4 free
Parking: Free
Phone: 954-921-3274
Website: www.artandculturecenter.org

Located in a historic Spanish-style mansion built in 1924, this center has exhibition galleries for visual art and a full schedule of art classes. Major shows of contemporary works are integrated with other events and programs to broaden the scope of community art appreciation and involvement.

Miami Beach

The allure of sand, surf, and sunny skies attracts tourists to this island resort, now a prime destination for sophisticated international travelers as well as cold-weather-weary Americans. The restoration of the classy art deco–style hotels, apartments, and shops and the rejuvenation of palm-lined Ocean Drive have created a playful, sophisticated atmosphere that captures the essence of south Florida.

153

ArtCenter/South Florida

Address: 800 Lincoln Road
   Miami Beach, FL 33139
Features: Classes, open access artists-in-residence studios
Hours: Gallery Monday and Wednesday 11–10, Thursday–Sunday 11–11
Admission: Free
Phone: 305-674-8278
Website: http://artcentersf.org

In the heart of the Arts District on Lincoln Road Mall, works by established and emerging artists are showcased in artists' studios carved from former shops and stores. This cluster of art activity proclaims its mission even in the fanciful tile floor and the handcrafted balcony overlooking some of the artists' studios and workrooms. Over forty juried artists share a dynamic spirit and vision in this energizing atmosphere of creativity and cultural diversity. Within the Arts District, other galleries, art-related businesses, cafés, and cultural institutions add depth and variety to this unique art community.

Bass Museum of Art

Address: 2121 Park Avenue
　　Miami Beach, FL 33139
Features: Lectures, concerts, films
Hours: Tuesday–Saturday 10–5,
　　Sunday 11–5
Admission: Adults $12, seniors $8,
　　students $6
Parking: Metered on-street parking
Phone: 305-673-7530
Website: http://bassmuseum.org

This elegant art deco building,
faced with cut coral stone from
the Florida Keys, stands in a
parklike setting. It was built in
the 1930s and is named for John
and Johanna Bass, who donated
their notable art collection to the
city in the 1960s. The permanent
collection spans the fourteenth
to the twentieth centuries, from
Rubens, Durer, and Daumier
to modern American masters.
Changing exhibitions feature
internationally distinguished
artists.

The Wolfsonian

Address: 1001 Washington Avenue
　　Miami Beach, FL 33139
Features: Museum shop, café, lec-
　　tures, films
Hours: Monday, Tuesday, Sat-
　　urday, Sunday 12–6, Thursday
　　and Friday 12–9
Admission: Adults $7 plus tax ,
　　seniors, students, and children
　　aged 6–12 $5 plus tax
Parking: Metered on-street
　　parking, parking garage
Phone: 305-531-1001
Website: http://wolfsonian.org

Energetically modern forms of

art—from graphics and sculpture
to home furnishings and public art
of the early twentieth century—are
handsomely displayed in this
spacious, seven-story building,
formerly a storage warehouse.
The core of this unique museum
is formed by more than seventy
thousand objects from the
Mitchell Wolfson Jr. Collection of
Decorative and Propaganda Arts,
which demonstrates the role of
design as an agent and expression
of change in the first half of the
twentieth century. Sleek art deco
objects, superb arts and crafts
furniture, forceful propaganda
and advertising posters, and
exhibits that celebrate modernity
and deal with urban industrialism
provide insightful glimpses of the
recent past. Ongoing programs
of lectures, films, symposia, and
collaborative events are presented
in conjunction with Florida
International University.

Jewish Museum of Florida

Address: 301 Washington Avenue
　　Miami Beach, FL 33139
Features: Museum store, films, lec-
　　tures, walking tours
Hours: Tuesday–Sunday 10–5
Admission: Adults $5, seniors
　　and students $5, children
　　under 6 free; admission free on
　　Saturday
Parking: Free
Phone: 305-672-5044
Website: http://jewishmuseum.com

The Jewish Museum of Florida
is housed in two adjacent former
historic synagogues—a restored
1936 art deco building and a

restored 1929 building that was Miami Beach's first Jewish congregation. The buildings are connected by a sky-lighted center court café. The museum collects, preserves, and interprets the Jewish experience in Florida from 1763 to the present in its core exhibit, *MOSAIC: Jewish Life in Florida,* with more than five hundred images and artifacts from all over the state. Among the surprises are Florida citrus crate labels in Yiddish and a marvelous dress covered in seashells worn at a Purim party in Jacksonville early in the twentieth century. Changing temporary art and history exhibits on related themes, a Collections & Research Center, Timeline Wall of Jewish history, and performance events and celebrations round out the rich offerings of this one-of-a-kind museum for visitors of all ages and backgrounds.

Miami

The cultural diversity of this tropical metropolis and its adjacent cities is reflected in the extraordinary scope of performing and visual arts centers and the wide range of special museums. Miami has been a magnet for tourists since Henry Flagler opened his Royal Palm Hotel in what is now the heart of the city's downtown area more than one hundred years ago. It now revels in its Latin American, Caribbean, and Hispanic connections. A place of enchantment to many, "the magic city" has survived many disasters, reinventing itself time and again.

Museum of Contemporary Art

Address: 770 Northeast
    125th Street
    North Miami, FL 33161
Features: Museum shop, gallery
    tours, lectures, films
Hours: Tuesday–Saturday 11–5,
    Sunday noon–5, last Friday of
    month 7 p.m.–10 p.m.
Admission: Adults $5, seniors and
    students $3
Parking: Free
Phone: 305-893-6211
Website: http://mocanomi.org

This splendid art museum is an architectural delight, with angled walls painted in complementary colors, water cascading into a low pool in front, rows of breezy palms, and plenty of space inside for the most ambitious shows. This is the place to discover new forms of artistic expression, revisit the modern masters in retrospective shows, and challenge your art appreciation boundaries.

Historical Museum of Southern Florida

Address: 101 West Flagler Street
    Miami, FL 33130
Features: Museum shop, research
    center, historic tours
Hours: Monday–Saturday 10–5,
    3rd Thursday 10–9, Sunday
    12–5

Admission: Adults $8, children $5, under age 6 free
Parking: Adjacent Cultural Center garage, $5 with validated ticket
Phone: 305-375-1492
Website: www.hmsf.org

Part of the Metro-Dade Cultural Center in downtown Miami designed by Philip Johnson, this state-of-the-art museum takes a keen and sweeping look at ten thousand years of history in southern Florida. Explore the past along a pathway of human progress, one that invites you to see, hear, and feel for yourself. Included are Calusa artifacts, displays relating to Seminole culture, an early homesteader's cottage, a restored 1925 trolley

car, and a tribute to the Roaring Twenties and art deco architecture. Thematic and visiting exhibits highlight special topics, and the museum sponsors historic walking, bus, and boat tours of the area.

Miami Art Museum

Address: 101 West Flagler Street
  Miami, FL 33130
Features: Museum shop, gallery talks, docent tours)
Hours: Tuesday–Friday 10–5, third Thursday of month open until 9, Saturday and Sunday noon–5

Admission: Adults $8, seniors $4
Parking: Adjacent Cultural Center garage, $5 with validated ticket
Phone: 305-375-3000
Website: www.miamiartmuseum. org

In keeping with Miami's distinctive cultural focus, the emphasis at the MAM, located in the Miami-Dade Cultural Center, is on exhibiting and collecting international art, particularly art of the Western Hemisphere created in the last half of the twentieth century. With many galleries of different sizes, a variety of artists, media, and themes create an interesting interplay of styles and impressions. Important shows are curated and presented to the public, enriching the vibrant cultural life of this semitropical metropolis.

NOTE: In 2011 Miami Art Museum will move to a new building in Museum Park on Biscayne Bay.

Vizcaya Museum and Gardens

Address: 3251 South Miami Avenue
  Miami, FL 33129
Features: Museum shop, café, guided tours
Hours: Daily 9:30–4:30
Admission: Adults $12, seniors, students, Miami-Dade residents

$9, children aged 6–12 $5, under age 6 free
Parking: Free
Phone: 305-250-9133
Website: www.vizcayamuseum.org

Plan to spend the day in this magnificent European-inspired estate on the edge of Biscayne Bay. Admire the splendid Renaissance pleasure palace built of native stone quarried on the property; savor the richness of the interiors, skillfully interpreted by knowledgeable docents; stroll slowly through the formal gardens, past fountains, classical statues, and fanciful grottos; sit awhile on the front plaza and imagine the Baroque-style stone barge floating away across the horizon. Although it appears to be centuries old, Vizcaya was actually built as a winter home by Chicago industrialist James Deering early in the twentieth century. Interpretive materials are available in several languages for the convenience of international visitors.

Miami Science Museum

Address: 3280 South Miami
   Avenue
   Miami, FL 33129
Features: Museum shop, food
   service, live science shows,
   planetarium, observatory,

picnic area
Hours: Daily 10–6
Admission: $13, under age 3 free
Parking: Free
Phone: 305-646-4200
Website: www.miamisci.org

Investigate the worlds of inner and outer space in this science museum that makes the physical and natural sciences accessible to visitors of all ages. Exhibits change often to bring new experiences, so you may encounter a Star Trek exhibition or the Dinosaurs of China, play virtual reality basketball, or log on to the multimedia stations in Cyber City. Reach for the stars in the award-winning Planetarium, visit the newest babies in the wildlife center, and take in a live science demonstration. MiaSci has plans for an expansive future when it moves to a new location in downtown Miami, so check the website for the latest developments.

Coconut Grove

Settled at the end of the nineteenth century by Bahamians and northerners seeking a healthy climate, this bayfront village has grown into a busy yachting, shopping, and entertainment center. The Dinner Key Marina is a magnet for boaters, and several large waterfront parks draw large crowds on weekends. The Coconut Grove Art Festival, held in February, is one of the largest in the South.

The Barnacle Historic State Park

Address: 3485 Main Highway
  Miami, FL 33133
Features: Guided tours
Hours: Friday–Monday 9–4; house
  tours at 10, 11:30, 1, and 2:30
  (limit 10 people per tour)
Admission: $1, under age 6 free
Parking: Metered on-street parking
Phone: 305-442-6866
Website: http://floridastateparks.
  org/thebarnacle

This unusual home was built
in 1891 by Commodore Ralph
Munroe, a noted boat designer and
yachtsman. Set back on a broad
lawn leading down to Biscayne
Bay, it was designed to blend
with the landscape and to make
the best of the tropical climate. A
naturalist and historian, Munroe
preserved much of the original
tropical hardwood hammock
between the house and the
entrance. Original furnishings in
the house and photographs taken
by Munroe provide rare glimpses
of pioneer life on Biscayne Bay.
The boathouse by the edge of the
bay is filled with tools and works
in progress, a reminder of a time
when boats were the principal
means of transportation. A replica
of one of Munroe's sailboats,
designed for the shallow waters of
the bay, is moored just offshore.

Fairchild Tropical Botanic Gardens

Address: 10901 Old Cutler Road
  Miami, FL 33156
Features: Plant, book, and gift
  shops; cafés; guided tram tours
Hours: Daily 9:30–4:30, Thursday
  6–9:30
Admission: Adults $20, seniors
  $15, children aged 6–17 $10,
  under age 5 free; fees higher
  on Thursday evening and for
  special events
Parking: Free
Phone: 305-667-1651
Website: http://fairchildgarden.org

Stroll along winding pathways
in this eighty-three-acre tropical
paradise, through the rain forest,
sunken garden, palm glade, vine
pergola, and other botanical
delights. Marvel at the exquisite
orchids and lush tropical plants in
the state-of-the-art conservatory
called Windows to the Tropics.
Relax and enjoy a tram ride to
view the largest tropical garden in
the continental United States. On
the grounds, a building constructed
of oolitic limestone by the Civilian
Conservation Corps (CCC)
contains a small museum devoted
to the activities of plant explorers:
horticulturists like David Fairchild
who roamed the world collecting
rare seeds and plant specimens.
Signs are in English and Spanish,
and interpretive materials in other
languages are available.

Coral Gables

Southwest of downtown Miami is a world of elegant living, planned early in the Florida land boom when Mediterranean-style architecture was at the height of its popularity. The centerpiece is the towering Biltmore Hotel, one of boom-time Florida's most elegant resorts. Other notable sites are the delightful Venetian Pool, the campus of the University of Miami, and Miracle Mile, the main shopping and commercial avenue.

Coral Gables Merrick House

Address: 907 Coral Way
   Coral Gables, FL 33134
Features: Guided tours
Hours: Wednesday–Sunday tours
   at 1, 2, and 3
Admission: Adults $5, seniors and
   students $3, children $1
Parking: Free
Phone: 305-460-5361
Website: http://www.coralgables.
   com/CGWeb/merrickhouse.
   aspx

This historic home, built between 1907 and 1910 and restored to the 1920s period, was the boyhood home of George E. Merrick, founder and developer of the city of Coral Gables. The house is

filled with the Merrick family's art, furniture, and personal treasures. Coral rock used to construct the house was quarried from the nearby Venetian Pool. Tropical gardens surrounding the house provide a perfect setting for this distinctive landmark.

Lowe Art Museum

Address: 1301 Stanford Drive
   Coral Gables, FL 33124
Features: Museum shop, picnic
   area
Hours: Tuesday, Wednesday,
   Friday, and Saturday 10–5,
   Thursday 12–7, Sunday 12–5
Admission: Adults $7, seniors and
   students $5, under age 12 free
Parking: Special metered spaces
   for museum visitors (purchase
   tokens inside)
Phone: 305-284-3535
Website: www.lowemuseum.org

A flaring green canopy shelters the entrance to this major art museum, which has expanded to provide generous galleries for displays of its broad and varied permanent collection. Major modern masters are on view, as well as exquisite pieces of Renaissance and baroque art from the Samuel H. Kress Collection and fine examples from the Lowe's Asian, African, pre-Columbian, and Native American collections. The oldest art museum in Miami-Dade County, located on the University of Miami campus, keeps up with the newest trends in art and provides lively changing exhibits. Complementary audio tours are available.

Greater Miami South

Native American hunting grounds in this area between the Everglades and Biscayne Bay gave way to productive winter vegetable farms and groves of oranges, limes, avocados, and mangoes early in the twentieth century. Residential communities have spread across fields and groveland, leaving only pockets of parks and nature preserves.

Florida International University, Frost Art Museum

Address: University Park, Southwest 107th Avenue and 8th Street
Miami, FL 33199
Hours: Monday, Tuesday, Thursday, Friday 10–5, Wednesday 10–9, Saturday and Sunday 12–4
Admission: Free
Parking: Metered spaces for visitors in Lot 6
Phone: 305-348-2890
Website: www.frostmuseum.org

The Patricia and Phillip Frost Art Museum moved into a new building on the FIU campus in 2008. The museum is recognized for its innovative exhibitions and programs and a collection that includes more than six thousand works of art. Shows of particular interest to the international community and works of students and faculty are regularly scheduled, and a lecture series invites the public to share with the university community a heightened appreciation for art. In the ArtPark, a collection of sculptures shares the sunshine with FIU students.

Miami-Dade College, Kendall Art Gallery

Address: 11011 Southwest 104th Street
Miami, FL 33176
Hours: Variable
Admission: Free
Parking: Free
Phone: 305-237-2322
Website: www.mdc.edu/kendall/art/default.asp

Herons and red-winged blackbirds make their home on the lakes of this suburban campus, surrounded by lush tropical vegetation. The Art Gallery, located in the southwest corner of the Fine Arts Building, presents stimulating and sometimes controversial exhibitions of contemporary regional, national, and international artists, with occasional strong shows by student artists.

Wings Over Miami Air Museum

Address: 14710 Southwest 128th Street, Kendall-Tamiami Airport
Miami, FL 33196
Features: Museum shop
Hours: Thursday–Sunday 10–5:30
Admission: Adults $9.95, seniors and children under 12 $5.95
Parking: Free
Phone: 305-233-5197
Website: www.weeksairmuseum.com

Located at the Kendall-Tamiami Airport, Wings Over Miami

displays and flies military and classic aircraft to share the history of flight by providing examples of operating historic aircraft. The museum pays tribute to those veterans and aviators who pioneered civilian and military aviation.

Florida Keys

Like gaudy beads cast on a turquoise sea, the Florida Keys are tied together by the overseas highway built on the roadbed of Henry Flagler's early twentieth-century "railroad that went to sea." Several sanctuaries have been established in the Keys to preserve their fragile and endangered natural and historical resources.

Crane Point Museum and Nature Center

Address: 5550 Overseas Highway
    Marathon, FL 33050
Features: Museum shop, picnic
    area, nature trail
Hours: Monday–Saturday 9–5,
    Sunday 12–5
Admission: Adults $8, seniors $6,
    students $4, under age 6 free
Parking: Free
Phone: 305-743-9100
Website: www.cranepoint.net
E-mail: info@cranepoint.net

The natural history and cultural diversity of the Florida Keys are presented in this museum complex located at Crane Point Hammock, midway down the Keys on Marathon. Tucked into the trees just off the highway, enter the modern building through the double doors faced with a remarkable metal-sculpted design evoking the natural wonders of the Keys. Innovative interpretive techniques include a walk-through coral reef simulation and explore the impact of Native Americans, pirates, wreckers, and the twentieth century on this subtropical archipelago. Don't miss the Wild Bird Rescue Center. In the Children's Museum, youngsters will enjoy meeting sea creatures in the touch tanks, and dressing as pirates and climbing aboard the replica pirate ship. A short walk through the hammock leads to the Adderley House, where you can enter the restored home of a Bahamian boatman who came to the Keys in the 1890s.

Pigeon Key

Address: Seven Mile Bridge, Mara-
    thon, FL
Mailing Address: P.O. Box 500130
    Marathon, FL 33050
Features: Museum shop, swim-
    ming, picnic area
Hours: Daily 10–4
Admission: Adults $11, children
    $8.50
Parking: Free
Phone: 305-743-5999
Website: www.pigeonkey.net

A cluster of wood-frame buildings on Pigeon Key comprises the only intact railroad village to survive from the early twentieth-century era when Henry Flagler built his Overseas Railway to Key West. Sections of the old railroad bridge still remain, and you may walk or bicycle over the bridge or board a ferry boat to the site. Park beside the silver-and-red railroad car, which serves as the visitor center at the Seven Mile Bridge, and board the ferry there. On Pigeon Key, a museum in the Assistant Bridge Tender's House displays artifacts and memorabilia from the railroad era. The beach is a nice place to have a picnic, enjoy a swim, or snorkel in the clear water.

Key West

Some people come to Key West just to see the sunset, and nowhere else is this event celebrated with such style and enthusiasm. Each evening, crowds of tourists, townspeople, vendors, and performers assemble on the broad concrete apron of the Mallory Square Pier facing the western sky, while yachts and sailboats cruise slowly by in the ship channel. Key West is also noted for its distinctive architecture, a blend of Caribbean-style comfort and Yankee ship-carpenter expertise, and restoration and preservation are a vital local concern.

The Oldest House and Garden

Address: 322 Duval Street
 Key West, FL 33040
Features: Museum shop
Hours: Thursday–Saturday 10–4
Admission: Free
Parking: Metered on-street parking
Phone: 305-294-9501
Website: http://www.oirf.org/
 museums/oldesthouse.htm

Wreckers played a vital part in the early boom-time economy of Key West. They were charged first with saving the crews of ships that wrecked on the treacherous reefs, then with salvaging as much of the cargoes and ships as possible. This house, built around 1829, belonged to Francis Watlington, a sea captain and professional wrecker. Delightful period furniture and decorative objects capture the affluent lifestyle of Captain Watlington and his family, and artifacts associated with the wrecking industry illuminate this important facet of Key West history. Interactive displays in the garden pavilion show the locations of some of the wrecks, and the old cook house, a small building a few steps from the rear porch, is a reminder of the challenge of food preparation in the nineteenth century.

Heritage House Museum

Address: 410 Caroline Street
 Key West, FL 33040
Hours: Monday–Saturday 10–5
Admission: guided tour $7, self-
 guided tour $5, children aged
 12–16 $1
Parking: Metered on-street parking
Phone: 305-296-3573
Website: http://heritagehouse
 museum.org

This Caribbean Colonial home

extends true island hospitality to its visitors. Leisurely tours introduce the notable Key West family who lived here for seven generations, furnishing their home with rare antiques, oriental art, artifacts collected by seagoing ancestors, and photos of their famous friends. One of the family's best-known friends was poet Robert Frost, who often stayed in a small guest cottage in a secluded tropical garden. For a very Key West experience, linger among the orchids and listen to a recording of Frost reading his poems.

Audubon House
and Tropical Gardens

Address: 205 Whitehead Street
    Key West, FL 33040
Features: Museum shop, audio
    tours
Hours: Daily 9:30–5
Admission: Adults $11, students
    $6.50 children aged 6–12 $6
Parking: Metered on-street
    parking, nearby parking garage
Phone: 305-294-2116
Website: www.audubonhouse.com

In the early nineteenth century, this three-story, white-frame structure was home to the large family of Captain John Geiger, a harbor pilot and master wrecker. Restored in the 1950s and exquisitely furnished in period antiques,

today it is closely associated with John James Audubon, who spent several months in the Keys in 1832, studying and drawing birds. Original Audubon prints are displayed and rare copies are for sale in the gallery. Children will enjoy the charming nursery furnished with antique toys and treasures. Ask about the audio tours in English and several other languages that allow visitors to absorb the history of the house at their own pace. A large garden filled with rare native and exotic plants encircles the house.

163

Mel Fisher Maritime Museum

Address: 200 Greene Street
    Key West, FL 33040
Features: Museum shop
Hours: Daily 8:30–5
Admission: Adults $11, students
    $9.50, children $6
Parking: Metered on-street
    parking, nearby parking garage
Phone: 305-294-2633
Website: http://melfisher.org

Those who have followed Mel Fisher and his diving team in their underwater search for the treasure of the Spanish fleet sunk by a hurricane in 1622 will enjoy seeing displays of recovered artifacts.

Exhibits focus on Fisher's quest for sunken Spanish treasure, particularly from the wreck of the *Nuestra Señora de Atocha*. In addition to the permanent displays related to early European maritime history in the Americas, there is a gallery for changing exhibits on the second floor of the museum.

Museum of Art and History at the Customs House

Address: 281 Front Street
　　Key West, FL 33040
Hours: Daily 9–5
Admission: Adults $10, seniors and residents $9, children and students $5, under age 6 free
Phone: 305-295-6616 x16
Website: www.kwahs.com

A striking landmark adjacent to Mallory Square, the imposing red-brick Customs House, built near the end of the nineteenth century, is now a must-see museum of Key West history and culture. A free video tour brings the many-layered history of the island city to life.

Little White House

Address: 111 Front Street
　　Key West, FL 33040
Features: Museum shop, guided tours
Hours: Daily 9–5
Admission: Adults $11, children $5
Parking: Metered on-street parking and Weston Hotel parking garage
Phone: 305-294-9911
Website: www.trumanlittle whitehouse.com

When President Harry Truman's doctor advised him to take a vacation in a warm climate, he chose the U.S. Navy base at Key West. The commandant's house was vacant, so it was redecorated and furnished for Truman and his family. He spent 175 days here during his presidency, between 1946 and 1952, relaxing from the formality of the White House in Washington, D.C. He liked it so much, he joked that he would like to move the nation's capital to Key West and stay there. The "Little White House" has been restored to Truman's era, complete with his famous poker table, cheerfully tasteful furnishings, and personal memorabilia. Tour guides bring Truman's tropical getaway alive with their insightful interpretations. If you are interested in tropical gardens, ask for a copy of the Botanical Tour brochure, and learn to identify exotic trees and shrubs as you stroll around the grounds.

Ernest Hemingway Home and Museum

Address: 907 Whitehead Street
Key West, FL 33040
Features: Book store, guided tours
Hours: Daily 9–5
Admission: Adults $11, children
$6
Parking: Limited on-street parking
Phone: 305-294-1136
Website: www.hemingwayhome.
com
E-mail: info@hemingwayhome.
com

Hemingway owned this home from 1931 to 1961 and wrote some of his most popular books in the studio behind the main house. The furnishings and memorabilia, including the author's typewriter and favorite chair, offer fascinating insights into his interests, exploits, travels, and lifestyle. Offspring of

his numerous cats still play among the trailing vines and tropical foliage in the yard, protected by the brick wall he built to shield himself from the attention of tourists. The palatial two-story residence, encircled with open verandas, was built of native rock in 1854 by Asa Tift, a wealthy Key West merchant.

Key West Lighthouse Museum

Address: 938 Whitehead Street
Key West, FL 33040
Features: Museum shop
Hours: Daily 9:30–4:30
Admission: Adults $10, seniors
and residents $9, children aged
6–12 $5, under age 6 free
Parking: Free parking in rear, off
Truman Avenue
Phone: 305-294-0012
Website: www.kwahs.com/light-
house.htm

Climb the eighty-eight steps to the top of this lighthouse for the best view of Key West and its surrounding blue-green waters. A lighthouse has stood on this spot since 1847, and this one was in use until 1969. The dedication to duty of the hardworking lightkeepers and their families comes to life in the restored keeper's house, filled with artifacts and items related to the maritime history of Key West.

Fort Zachary Taylor Historic State Park

Physical address: End of Southard
Street on Truman Annex
Mailing address: P.O. Box 6560
Key West, FL 33041
Features: Guided tours, picnic area
and beach in adjacent park
Hours: Daily 8–sunset, guided

tours at 12 and 2
Admission: Free
Parking: Per vehicle, $6, each
    additional person $.50
Phone: 305-292-6713
Website: http://floridastate
    parks.org/forttaylor

This low-lying fort on the southwestern tip of the island was built in 1845, shortly after Florida became a state. It was originally surrounded by water, connected to land by a causeway, and had a desalination plant to convert sea water to drinking water. The extraordinary brickwork is being restored, and many of the cannons, buried in sand inside the gun rooms to strengthen the structure during the Spanish-American War, have been excavated. Tours led by park rangers help visitors understand the role of the fort and its evolution. The adjacent beach within the state park is popular with sunbathers, swimmers, and snorkelers.

East Martello
Museum and Gallery

Address: 3501 South Roosevelt
    Boulevard
    Key West, FL 33040
Features: Museum shop
Hours: Daily 9:30–4:30
Admission: Adults $6, seniors
    and residents $5, children
    and students $3
Parking: Free
Phone: 305-296-3913
Website: http://kwahs.com/
    Martello.htm

Constructed in 1862 during the Civil War, this brick fortress now serves as a historical museum and art gallery. The vaulted brick ceilings of the gun rooms and curved walls of the citadel tower enhance the charm of an eclectic collection of artifacts that highlight Key West's haunted past.

List of Contacts

If you are planning your trip in advance, these contacts can provide you with up-to-date information, colorful vacation guides, detailed calendars of events, useful maps, lists of accommodations, valuable details about attractions, and so on. Most counties have a visitors and convention bureau or a tourist development council. If neither is listed, you will find a listing for either the chamber of commerce or the county commission. Please note that some counties have divided their tourism offices into two or three regional offices and some have combined their tourism information services with those of other counties.

Each entry is headed by the county name and section of Florida that corresponds to the regional divisions used in this guide.

Alachua County-Northeast Florida
Alachua County Visitor and
Convention Bureau
30 East University Avenue
Gainesville, FL 32601
Phone: 352-374-5260
Fax: 352-338-3213
Website: www.visitgainesville.net

Baker County-Northeast Florida
Baker County Chamber of
Commerce
20 West Macclenny Avenue
Macclenny, FL 32063
Phone: 904-259-6433
Fax: 904-259-2737
Website: www.bakerchamberfl.com

Bay County-Northwest Florida
Panama City Beach Convention and
Visitors Bureau
Post Office Box 9473
Panama City Beach, FL 32417-9473
Phone: 850-233-5070, 800-553-133
Website: http://thebeachloversbeach.
com

Bradford County-Northeast Florida
Bradford County Tourist
Development Council
202 Walnut Street
Starke, FL 32091
Phone: 904-964-5278
Fax: 904-964-2863
Website: http://.northfloridachamber.
com

Brevard County-Central East Florida
Cocoa Beach Convention and
Visitors Bureau
400 Fortenberry Road
Merritt Island, FL 32952
Phone: 321-454-2022
Fax: 321-383-0107
Website: www.visitcocoabeach.com

Florida Space Coast
Office of Tourism
Brevard County Tourist
Development Council
430 Brevard Avenue, Suite 150
Cocoa Village, FL 32922
Phone: 877-572-3224
Fax: 321-433-4476
Website: www.space-coast.com

Melbourne-Palm Bay Area Chamber of Commerce
1005 East Strawbridge Avenue
Melbourne, FL 32955
Phone: 321-724-5400
Fax: 321-725-2093
Website: www.melpb-chamber.org

Broward County-Southeast Florida
Greater Fort Lauderdale Convention and Visitors Bureau
100 East Broward Boulevard, Suite 200
Fort Lauderdale, FL 33301
Phone: 954-765-4466, 800-22-SUNNY
Fax: 954-765-4467
Website: www.sunny.org

Calhoun County-Northwest Florida
Calhoun County Chamber of Commerce
20816 Central Avenue, Suite 2
Blountstown, FL 32424
Phone: 850-674-4519
Fax: 850-674-4962
Website: www.calhounco.org

Charlotte County-Southwest Florida
Charlotte Harbor and Gulf Islands Visitors Bureau
18501 Murdock Circle, Suite 502
Port Charlotte, FL 33948
Phone: 941-743-1900, (toll-free) 800-652-6090
Website: www.charlotteharbortravel.com

Citrus County-Central West Florida
Citrus County Visitors Bureau
9225 West Fishbowl Drive
Homosassa, FL 34448
Phone: 352-628-9305
Fax: 352-628-0703
Website: www.visitcitrus.com

Clay County-Northeast Florida
Clay County Tourist Development Council
1734 Kingsley Avenue
Orange Park, FL 32073
Phone: 904-394-7401
Fax: 904-264-0070
Website:www.claytourism.com

Collier County-Southwest Florida
Marco Island and the Everglades Convention and Visitors Bureau
3050 North Horseshoe Drive, Suite 218
Naples, FL 34104
Phone: 239-403-2384
Fax: 941-403-2404
Website:www.paradisecoast.com

Columbia County-Northeast Florida
Columbia County Tourist Development Council
263 Northwest Lake City Avenue
Lake City, FL 32055
Phone: 9386-758-1397
Website: www.springsrus.com

DeSoto County-Central West Florida
DeSoto County Tourism Development Council
16 South Volusia Avenue
Arcadia, FL 34266
Phone: 863-494-4033
Fax: 863-494-3312
Website: www.desotochamber.net

Dixie County-Northwest Florida
Dixie County Chamber of Commerce
Post Office Box 547
Cross City, FL 32628
Phone: 352-498-5454
Website: www.dixiecounty.org

Duval County-Northeast Florida
Jacksonville and the Beaches
Convention and Visitors Bureau
550 Water Street, Suite 1000
Jacksonville, FL 32202
Phone: 904-798-9111, 800-733-2668
Fax: 904-798-9103
Website:www.jaxcvb.com

Escambia County-Northwest Florida
Pensacola Convention and Visitors
Information Center
1401 East Gregory Street
Pensacola, FL 32501
Phone: 800-874-1234
Fax: 850-432-8211
Website: www.visitpensacola.com

Flagler County-Northeast Florida
Flagler County Chamber of
Commerce
20 Airport Road
Palm Coast, FL 32164
Phone: 386-437-0106, 800-881-1022
Fax: 386-437-5700
Website: www.flaglerchamber.org

Franklin County-Northwest Florida
Apalachicola Bay Chamber of
Commerce
122 Commerce Street
Apalachicola, FL 32320
Phone: 850-653-9419
Fax: 850-653-8219
Website: www.apalachicolabay.org

**Carrabelle Area Chamber of
Commerce**
Post Office Drawer DD
Carrabelle, FL 32322
Phone: 850-697-2585
Website: www.carrabelle.org

Gadsden County-Northwest Florida
Gadsden County Chamber of
Commerce
Post Office Box 389
Quincy, FL 32353
Phone: 850-627-9231
Website: www.gadsdencc.com

Gilchrist County-Northwest Florida
Gilchrist County Chamber of
Commerce
220 South Main Street
Trenton, FL 32693
Phone: 352-463-3467
Fax: 352-463-3469
Website: www.gilchristcounty.com

Gulf County-Northwest Florida
Gulf County Chamber of Commerce
155 Captain Fred's Place
Port St. Joe, FL 32456
Phone: 850-227-1223
Fax: 850-227-9684
Website: www.gulfchamber.org

Hamilton County-Northwest Florida
Hamilton County Tourism
Development Council
Post Office Box 1056
Jasper, FL 32052
Phone: 904-792-6828
Website: www.
hamiltoncountyonline.com

Hardee County-Central Florida
Hardee County Chamber of
Commerce
Post Office Box 683
Wauchula, FL 33873
Phone: 863-773-6967
Website: www.hardeecc.com

Hendry County-Southeast Florida
Hendry County Board of County
Commissioners
Post Office Box 1760
La Belle, FL 33975
Phone: 863-675-5220
Website: http://www.hendryflorida.
com/BOCC.htm

**Hernando County-Central West
Florida**
Hernando County Tourist
Development Council
30305 Cortez Boulevard
Brooksville, FL 34602
Phone: 352-754-4405
Fax: 352-754-4406
Website: www.co.hernando.fl.us/visit

Highlands County-Central Florida
Highlands County Convention and
Visitors Bureau
2113 U.S. 27 South
Sebring, FL 33870
Phone: 863-386-1316
Fax: 863-545-6021
Website: www.highlandscvb.com

**Hillsborough County-Central West
Florida**
Tampa/Hillsborough Convention
and Visitors Association
41 East Jackson Street, Suite 2100
Tampa, FL 33602
Phone: 813-223-1111
Fax: 813-229-6616
Website: www.visittampabay.com

Holmes County-Northwest Florida
Holmes County Chamber of
Commerce
106 East Byrd Avenue
Bonifay, FL 32425
Phone: 850-547-4682
Fax: 850-547-4206
Website:www.holmescountyonline.
com

**Indian River County-Central East
Florida**
Indian River County Tourist Division
Marketing Director
1216 21st Street
Vero Beach, FL 32960
Phone: 772-567-3491
Website: www.indianriverchamber.
com

Jackson County-Northwest Florida
Marianna Chamber of Commerce
Post Office Box 130
Marianna, FL 32447
Phone: 850-482-8060
Fax: 850-482-8002
Website: www.jacksoncounty.com

Jefferson County-Northwest Florida
Monticello/Jefferson County
Chamber of Commerce
420 West Washington Street
Monticello, FL 32344
Phone: 850-997-5552
Website: www.monticellojeffersonfl.
com

Lafayette County-Northwest Florida
Lafayette County Chamber of
Commerce
Executive Director
Post Office Box 416
Mayo, FL 32066
Phone: 904-294-2705

Lake County-Central Florida
Lake County Convention and
Visitors Bureau
20763 U.S. Highway 27
Groveland, FL 34736
Phone: 352-429-3673
Fax: 352-429-4870
Website: www.lakecountyfl.gov/
visitors

Lee County-Southwest Florida
Lee County Visitor and Convention
Bureau
1280 University Drive, Suite550
Fort Myers, FL 33907
Phone: 239-338-3500
Fax: 239-334-1106
Website: www.leevcb.com

Leon County-Northwest Florida
Tallahassee Area Convention and
Visitors Bureau
106 East Jefferson Street
Tallahassee, FL 32301
Phone: 850-606-2305, 800-628-
2866
Fax: 850-606-2301
Website: www.visittallahasee.com

Levy County-Northwest Florida
Nature Coast Business Development
Council
Post Office Box 1112
Bronson, Florida 32621
Phone: (352) 486-5470
Fax: (352) 486-5471
Website: www.naturecoast.org

Liberty County-Northwest Florida
Liberty County Chamber of
Commerce
Post Office Box 523
Bristol, FL 32321
Phone: 850-643-2359
Website: www.libertycountyflorida.
com

Madison County-Northwest Florida
Madison County Chamber of
Commerce
125 Northeast Range Avenue
Madison, FL 32340
Phone: 850-973-2788
Fax: 850-973-8864
Website: www.madisonfl.org

**Manatee County-Central West
Florida**
Bradenton Area Convention and
Visitors Bureau
Post Office Box 1000
Bradenton, FL 34206
Phone: 941-729-9177
Fax: 941-729-1820
Website: www.floridaislandbeaches.
org

Marion County-Central Florida
Ocala/Marion County Chamber of
Commerce
110 East Silver Springs Boulevard
Ocala, FL 34470-6613
Phone: 352-629-8051
Fax: 352-6293529
Website: www.ocalacc.com

Martin County-Southeast Florida
Stuart/Martin County Chamber of
Commerce
1650 South Kanner Highway
Stuart, FL 34994-7199
Phone: 727-287-1088
Fax: 727-220-3437
Website: www.goodnature.org

**Miami-Dade County-Southeast
Florida**
701 Brickell Avenue, Suite 2700
Miami, FL 33131
Phone: 305-539-3000, 800-933-
8448
Website: www.gmcvb.com

Monroe County-Southwest Florida
Monroe County Tourist
Development Council
102 White Street, Suite102
Key West, FL 33040
Phone: 305-296-1552
Fax: 305-296-0788
Website: www.fla-keys.com

Nassau County-Northeast Florida
Amelia Island Tourist Development
Council
961687 Gateway Boulevard, Suite G
Amelia Island, FL 32034
Phone: (toll-free) 800-2AMELIA
Fax: 904-261-6997
Website: www.amelianature.com

**Greater Nassau County Chamber of
Commerce**
Post Office Box 98
Callahan, FL 32011
Phone: 904-879-1441
Fax: 904-879-4033
Website: www.greaternassaucounty.
com

Okaloosa County-Northwest Florida
Emerald Coast Convention and
Visitors Bureau
Post Office Box 609
Fort Walton Beach, FL 32549-0609
Phone: 800-322-3319
Website: www.destin-fwb.com

**Okeechobee County-Central East
Florida**
Okeechobee County Tourist
Development Council
499 Northwest 5th Avenue
Okeechobee, FL 34972
Phone: 863-763-5785
Fax: 863-763-3959
Website: www.okeechobee-tdc.com

Orange County-Central Florida
Orlando/Orange County Convention
and Visitors Bureau
6700 Forum Drive, Suite 100
Orlando, FL 32821
Phone: 800-972-3304
Website: www.orlandoinfo.com

Osceola County-Central Florida
Kissimmee/St. Cloud Convention
and Visitors Bureau
1925 Irlo Bronson Memorial
Highway
Kissimmee, FL 34744
Phone: 407-944-2400
Website: www.floridakiss.com

**Palm Beach County-Southeast
Florida**
Palm Beach County Convention and
Visitors Bureau
1555 Palm Beach Lakes Boulevard,
Suite 204
West Palm Beach, FL 33401
Phone: 561-233-300, 800-833-5733
Fax: 561-233-3009
Website: www.palmbeachfl.com

Pasco County-Central West Florida
Pasco County Office of Tourism
7530 Little Road, Suite 340
New Port Richey, FL 34654
Phone: 800-842-1873
Website: www.visitpasco.net

**Pinellas County-Central West
Florida**
St. Petersburg/Clearwater Area
Convention and Visitors Bureau
805 58th Street, N, Suite 2-200
Clearwater, FL 33760
Phone: 727-464-7200, 800-352-
3224
Website: www.stpete-clearwater.com

Polk County-Central Florida
Central Florida Visitor and
Convention Bureau
600 West Broadway, Suite 300
Bartow, FL 33830
Phone: 800-828-7655
Website: www.visitcentralflorida.org

Putnam County-Northeast Florida
Putnam County Chamber of
Commerce
Post Office Box 550
Palatka, FL 32178-0550
Phone: 386-328-1503
Fax: 386-328-7076
Website: www.
putnamcountychamber.org

St. Johns County-Northeast Florida
St. Johns County Visitors and
Convention Bureau
88 Riberia Street, Suite 250
St. Augustine, FL 32084
Phone: (toll-free) 800-653-2489
Website: www.getaway4florida.com

**St. Lucie County-Central East
Florida**
St. Lucie County Tourist
Development Council
2300 Virginia Avenue
Fort Pierce, FL 34982
Phone: 800-344-8443
Website: www.visitstluciefla.com

**Santa Rosa County-Northwest
Florida**
Gulf Breeze Area Chamber of
Commerce
409 Gulf Breeze Parkway
Gulf Breeze, FL 32562
Phone: 850-932-7888
Fax: 850-934-4601
Website: www.gulfbreezechamber.
com

**Santa Rosa County Chamber of
Commerce**
5247 Stewart Street
Milton, FL 32570
Phone: 850-623-2339
Website: www.srcchamber.com

**South Santa Rosa County Visitor
Information Center**
8543 Navarre Parkway
Navarre, FL 32566
Phone: 850-939-2691, 800-480-
7263
Fax: 850-939-0085
Website: www.beaches-rivers.com

**Sarasota County-Central West
Florida**
Sarasota Convention and Visitors
Bureau
701 North Tamiami Trail
Sarasota, FL 34236
Phone: 941-957-1877, 800-522-
9799
Fax: 941-951-2956
Website: www.sarasotafl.org

Seminole County-Central Florida
Seminole County Convention and
Visitors Bureau
1230 Douglas Avenue, Suite 116
Longwood, FL 32779
Phone: 407-665-2900, 800-800-
7832
Fax: 407-665-2920
Website: www.visitseminole.com

Sumter County-Central Florida
Sumter County Chamber of
Commerce
Post Office Box 100
Lake Panasoffkee, FL 33538
Phone: 352-793-3099
Website: www.sumtercountytoday.
com

Suwannee County-Northwest Florida

Suwannee County Chamber of Commerce
Post Office Drawer C
Live Oak, FL 32064
Phone: 386-362-3071
Fax: 386-362-4758
Website: www.suwanneechamber.com

Taylor County-Northwest Florida

Perry-Taylor County Chamber of Commerce
428 North Jefferson Street
Perry, FL 32348
Phone: 850-584-5366
Website: www.taylorcountychamber.com

Union County-Northeast Florida

North Florida Regional Chamber of Commerce
100 East Call Street
Starke, FL 32091
Phone: 904-964-5278
Fax: 904-964-2863
Website: www.northfloridachamber.com

Volusia County-Central East Florida

Daytona Beach Area Convention and Visitors Bureau
126 East Orange Avenue
Daytona Beach, FL 32115
Phone: 386-255-0415
Fax: 386-255-5478
Website: www.daytonabeachcvb.org

Southeast Volusia Tourism

Advertising Authority
2238 State Road 44
New Smyrna Beach, FL 32168
Phone: 386-428-1600

Wakulla County-Northwest Florida

Wakulla County Tourist Development Council
Phone: 850-984-3966
Website: www.wakullacounty.org

Walton County-Northwest Florida

South Walton Tourist Development Council
Post Office Box 1248
Santa Rosa Beach, FL 32459
Phone: 800-822-6877
Fax: 850-267-3943
Website: www.beachesofsouthwalton.com

Walton County Chamber of Commerce

95 Circle Drive
DeFuniak Springs, FL 32435
Phone: 850-892-3191
Fax: 850-892-9688
Website: www.waltoncountychamber.com

Washington County-Northwest Florida

Washington County Chamber of Commerce
Post Office Box 457
Chipley, FL 32428
Phone: 850-638-4157
Fax: 850-638-8770
Website: www.washcomall.com

County Groups

Alachua, Bradford, Columbia,
Dixie, Gilchrist, Hamilton,
Lafayette, Madison, Suwannee,
Taylor, and Union Counties
The Original Florida
Post Office Box 1300
Lake City, FL 32036-1300
Phone: 1-877-746-4778
Website: www.originalflorida.org

Broward, Collier, Glades, Hendry,
and Hillsborough Counties
Seminole Tribe of Florida
6300 Stirling Road
Hollywood, FL 33024
Phone: 800-683-7800
Website: www.seminoletribe.com

Citrus, Dixie, Hernando, Jefferson,
Levy, Pasco, Taylor, and Wakulla
Counties, and City of Dunnellon
Florida's Nature Coast
30305 Cortez Boulevard
Brooksville, FL 34602
Phone: 352-754-4405
Fax: 352-754-4406

More Websites

In addition to the websites listed
in the previous section and those
included with individual attractions,
we discovered some others that
may provide you with more useful
information.

Florida Association of Museums
www.flamuseum.org

Florida Office of Cultural, Historical
and Information Programs
www.flheritage.com

Florida Festival and Fair Calendar
www.southfest.com/florida

Florida Railroad Museums
www.railmuseums.com/namerica/
FLORIDA

Index
by Attraction (City)

Index
by Category

Index

Photo Credits